Praise for *The Social Emotional Classroom*

"*The Social Emotional Classroom* provides step-by-step plans and action-oriented activities for the busy educator to use with their students. District administrators will want to make this book a 'must read' for all their classroom teachers!"

—**Timothy Hagan**,
President & CEO, Education Associates

"Teachers have learned well the importance of social emotional learning and this book provides excellent guidelines to navigate this critical area. Well-articulated descriptions, charts for assessing SEL health, and creative and helpful suggestions for the school environment make *The Social Emotional Classroom* a valuable resource for any educator."

—**Dr. Maria Cleary**,
President of Readeezy and
former school superintendent

"For educators looking to cut through all the noise around SEL, *The Social Emotional Classroom* provides a straightforward and practical guide to bring SEL into your classroom. Based on extensive research, this guide is easily skimmable to help busy educators get just the information they need when they need it to support their students as well as themselves."

—**Kate Finnefrock**,
education executive with over 20 years'
experience building products for educators

"This book is rather timely. It comes at a time in history when the world is returning to a new normal after a raging pandemic that has established social emotional learning as a necessity in education. It will empower educators world-wide on how to transform their classrooms into safe, social emotional spaces that cultivate well-being, enable holistic development, and contribute to building a kinder world."

—**Nandini Chatterjee Singh**,
cognitive neuroscientist,
Senior National Program Officer, UNESCO MGIEP

The Social Emotional Classroom

The Social Emotional Classroom

A NEW WAY TO NURTURE STUDENTS AND UNDERSTAND THE BRAIN

Anna-Lisa Mackey M.Ed.
Melissa Ragan

JOSSEY-BASS™
A Wiley Brand

Published by Jossey-Bass, a Wiley Brand
111 River St
Hoboken, New Jersey 07030
www.josseybass.com

Jossey-Bass books and products are available through most bookstores. To contact Jossey-Bass directly call our Customer Care Department within the U.S. at 800-956-7739, outside the U.S. at 317-572-3986, or fax 317-572-4002.

Wiley publishes in a variety of print and electronic formats and by print-on-demand. Some material included with standard print versions of this book may not be included in e-books or in print-on-demand. If this book refers to media such as a CD or DVD that is not included in the version you purchased, you may download this material at http://booksupport.wiley.com. For more information about Wiley products, visit www.wiley.com.

Library of Congress Cataloging-in-Publication Data

Names: Mackey, Anna-Lisa, author. | Ragan, Melissa, author.
Title: The social emotional classroom : a new way to nurture students and understand the brain / Anna-Lisa Mackey, Melissa Ragan.
Description: Hoboken, Jew Jersey : Jossey-Bass, 2022. | Includes bibliographical references and index.
Identifiers: LCCN 2022000567 (print) | LCCN 2022000568 (ebook) | ISBN 9781119814320 (paperback) | ISBN 9781119814337 (adobe pdf) | ISBN 9781119814344 (epub)
Subjects: LCSH: Affective education. | Emotions and cognition. | Emotions in children.
Classification: LCC LB1072 .M34 2022 (print) | LCC LB1072 (ebook) | DDC 370.15/34—dc23/eng/20220215
LC record available at https://lccn.loc.gov/2022000567
LC ebook record available at https://lccn.loc.gov/2022000568

Cover Design: Wiley
Cover Image: © Wavebreakmedia/Getty Images; Courtesy of Maria O'Leary; Courtesy of Nicole Mamdani, Face 2 Face photography

SKY10034645_060222

For my husband, Glen,
and our girls, Faith, Amanda, and Nicole

Anna-Lisa Mackey

~

For my husband Alex, and our children,
Sam, Alex, Lucy, and Molly

Melissa Ragan

CONTENTS

ABOUT THE AUTHORS

Anna-Lisa Mackey is the CEO of PATHS Program, LLC, a publisher and distributor of award-winning social emotional learning programs for students and teachers. Anna-Lisa has worked with children at risk of developing serious behavior problems as well as training and implementing the PATHS® programs throughout the world for over 20 years. She has also spoken about SEL at national conferences including the Innovative School Summit (US), Atlantic Summer Institute (Canada), and Blueprints Conference (US).

Melissa Ragan is a former high school English teacher, and for the past 15 years she has written and delivered professional development resources. She has written for companies including Scholastic, co-created a family engagement program for HMH, and authored a high school transition and social emotional learning curriculum for an ed-tech startup. Melissa has spoken at national conferences on topics focused on English learners, parent engagement, and special education.

ACKNOWLEDGMENTS

This book would not have been possible without the input from the hundreds of teachers and administrators who spoke with us fearlessly and honestly, including Priti Ahuja, Katie Bruce, Danny Lackey, Terri-Anne Larry, Ann McGreevey, Katie Suriano, and Michelle Thompson. We're so grateful for the work you do every day.

We are also grateful for the guidance of the team at Wiley, especially Amy Fandrei, our amazing editor, Pete Gaughan, Sunny Collins, Selvakumaran Rajendiran, and Evelyn Wellborn.

Finally, we couldn't have done it without the support of our families who encouraged us through the entire development process.

Anna-Lisa Mackey and Melissa Ragan

INTRODUCTION

In 2019, we began our work on a brand-new social emotional learning curriculum for middle school students. In 2020, within a month of going to print with our new program, we discovered the work of Dr. Lisa Feldman Barrett and her book *How Emotions Are Made.* Dr. Barrett's new research changed everything we *thought* we knew about emotions. As we learned more, we made the decision to literally stop the presses so we could update the pedagogical approach of our new curriculum with the latest research and innovations on emotions and the brain; here's why.

You are probably familiar with the classical view of emotions and the brain, which has informed Social Emotional Learning (SEL) to date. This view posits that there are specific areas of the brain that are involved in emotions (specifically the prefrontal cortex, hypothalamus, and the amygdala). These areas of the brain work in concert. The amygdala reacts to the emotion that we are experiencing and sends a signal to the hypothalamus, triggering a physical response. This release of hormones is responsible for the body's response, specifically in instances of fear, such as an increased heartbeat or dilated pupils. This theory, often referred to as the "fight or flight response" was first identified in the 1920s.

While this theory was first thought to help people to perform better in stressful situations, one caveat is that it is not always accurate. It's easy for your brain to get tricked. For instance, walking through the woods and spotting a branch that you mistake for a snake.

In addition, this theory doesn't take into account human variation. Specifically, the fact that all people are different. What makes one person feel scared, such as visiting a haunted house, may make another person feel exhilarated. What makes someone feel happy, like celebrating a birthday, can make another feel sad.

Cultural differences also play a part. We could write an entire book about how different cultures view emotions and about culture display rules, but suffice to say, while emotions might be universal, expressing and interpreting emotions can differ by culture. In fact, some cultures have words for emotions that we don't even identify in English. We'll go into more detail on this in Chapter 2, "Self-Awareness."

The classical theory says that the prefrontal cortex is responsible for thinking, problem-solving, and planning. The main job often ascribed to the prefrontal cortex is to calm the amygdala in these fight or flight situations. The ability to calm oneself is called self-regulation. The classical view suggests that people have difficulty exercising self-control, that their emotions can hijack their behaviors. However, we now know that people can, in fact, maintain control of the way they react to their feelings and emotions. This ability to exert control over your emotions is a learned behavior and one that can be taught. When an individual is able to exert this self-control over their emotions, they can be more successful in life.

The classical view of the brain also holds that there are specific facial expressions and body language that correspond to various emotions and that they are universal in nature. In order to truly be effective in interpersonal interactions, it is our responsibility to learn how to "read" these expressions and understand their meaning. This understanding of the brain and how it works comes from the science of neurobiology. Based on a large meta-analysis of the research, we now know that there is little evidence to support this classical view of emotion. There are several reasons—inability to replicate the results of previous research, faulty assumptions, and inconsistencies. In addition, with the advent of improved imaging with functional Magnetic Resonance Imaging (fMRI), this classical view of the workings of the brain has been shown to be based on stereotypes, misinterpretation of research results, and/or faulty research design.

Despite common misconceptions, emotions do not have markers or specific, recognizable, universal facial features. Take the experience of "happy" for instance. Sometimes we smile, sometimes we cry, sometimes we show nothing on our face to indicate to others how we feel. When we say we are happy, we are not experiencing all the kinds of happiness that can be experienced on the happiness spectrum. We are experiencing one example of happiness, or an instance of the emotion happy. To say that happiness is experienced in only one way is, by instinct, incorrect because we have felt happy in many different situations. What instance of happiness do you feel at your birthday party? What instance of happiness do you feel at someone else's birthday party? Are they the same or different? In both these examples, the brain is predicting the sort of happy concept that it thinks is appropriate in the moment. And it does it so rapidly that we do not perceive this guessing game at work.

Constructionism is not necessarily a new theory. It is based on ideas dating back to ancient Greece. However, today's Constructionist approach comprises several ideas. One, that variation is the norm not the exception. And two, that our experience of emotion or our emotion concepts are based on our social context. There are three aspects of constructionism that also participate in the theory of constructed emotion: social construction, which focuses on how we interact with the world; psychological construction, which focuses on our thoughts and feelings; and neuro construction, which contributes to our understanding about how the brain is wired. These new findings have led to a new view of emotions and the brain called the theory of constructed emotion. This theory, coined by neuroscientist Dr. Feldman Barrett, holds that the entire brain as well as the body is involved in emotion!

Learning emotions is similar to language acquisition. Even before birth, the brain begins to receive information based on experiences. In every experience, the brain perceives sensations from the body, and it attempts to categorize this information. As we grow and have more experiences, we continue to categorize them and/or add new information to these categories. These categories are called concepts. Remember the scene in the Disney/PIXAR movie *Inside Out* where the emotions are in Riley's memory vault? You can think of all those marble-like capsules as concepts.

The information that the brain receives from the body is called interoception, which is information from the senses that the brain interprets into concepts. Language is an important part of concept formation, which, as we learned, represents past experiences. As more concepts are formed, the brain begins to make predictions based on the interoceptive information and the context or situation in which you find yourself. These concepts are how the brain makes meaning of all the sensations and input it receives. Sometimes, the prediction of meaning results in an emotion like happy, sad, mad, etc. Sometimes, these predictions can be wrong.

Meanwhile, there's another important influence in how your brain's predictions are made—your body budget.

The entire purpose of the brain is to keep you alive. To do so, the body must be healthy, which means it has to be kept in balance—not too cold, not too hot, not too hungry, not too thirsty, etc. This is referred to as the body budget. Your body budget can have a significant impact on your emotions. Have you ever tried having a difficult conversation when you're hungry? Or overreacted about something because you were not feeling well? The effect of an unbalanced body budget's impact on your brain's predictions can't be overlooked.

These new findings have significant consequences for social emotional learning in the classroom. With the new interest and focus on including SEL in schools, it's now more important than ever to understand the new science and research!

In this book, we'll discuss the new research of the brain and emotion in connection with social emotional learning in education. We will connect this new understanding to the five SEL domains (as defined by CASEL, the Collaborative for Academic, Social, and Emotional Learning) to help teachers explicitly embed social emotional learning into their everyday practice while simultaneously improving their own knowledge.

In each chapter, you'll learn about the SEL competencies, the constructionist theory, as well as new research on the subject. You'll also find plenty of real-world examples you can put into practice, gain resources to put the practice into action, and finally reflect on what you've learned. We look forward to hearing your questions, feedback, and success stories. Please feel free to contact Anna-Lisa Mackey at CEO@pathsprogram.com and Melissa Ragan at raganmelissa@gmail.com

Note: Some of the resources shown or mentioned in this book are available for download, from the book's web page at http://www.wiley.com/go/socialemotionalclassroom.

CHAPTER 1

Social Emotional Learning

What Is Social Emotional Learning? (And Why Is It Important?)

Social emotional learning (SEL) is a lot like politics. Everyone has an opinion about it, and everyone thinks they are right. While there is some gray area in the realm of SEL, some of the ideas people have about SEL simply aren't accurate. Part of that is due to common misunderstandings, but many people also are not aware of the new information and research that is available and can be used to inform their understanding of SEL.

For this book, we surveyed hundreds of educators all over the world. Our goal was to gain a better perspective of how teachers, administrators, counselors, and other education professionals understand and view social emotional learning (SEL). Their responses did not surprise us. In fact, it illustrated why this work is so important. For example, if you ask ten different people, you'll get ten different definitions for SEL.

While there are no current national standards for social emotional learning, the Collaborative for Academic, Social, and Emotional Learning (CASEL) is considered the leading authority for SEL in the United States. They define SEL as: *"The process through which all young people and adults acquire and apply the knowledge, skills, and attitudes to develop healthy identities, manage emotions and achieve personal and collective goals, feel and show empathy for others, establish and maintain supportive relationships, and make responsible and caring decisions."*

CASEL has established five core domains and connected competencies for social emotional learning: self-awareness, self-management, social awareness, decision making, and relationship skills. Throughout this book, we'll review each competency, and explain how the new constructionist view of the brain impacts teaching the SEL practice in the classroom.

You'll also find examples of SEL practices in action for each domain from teachers like you, learn practical SEL activities you can implement in the classroom, see SEL lesson plans in every subject area, and reflect on what you've learned.

Why Is SEL Important?

Believe it or not, social emotional learning is controversial!

One Facebook ad about an SEL curriculum, for example, led to comments such as: *"Keep that social justice crap to yourself!"* At least one large research organization has called SEL "kooky" and "Orwellian." Another called it a "fad" and "faux psychology." And parent groups in some states have worked to ban SEL because its goal is to "divert all educational resources toward political activism and indoctrination" and linked it to critical race theory.

One blogger accused schools of using SEL to "tell children how to think and feel" and in one state, SEL was compared to "dystopian behavior control" by its education leaders. However, SEL doesn't tell students how to think or feel. It teaches them how to regulate their emotions when they feel uncomfortable as well as appropriate behaviors for some emotions and feelings.

Some parent groups have expressed concern over what content will be included in the SEL lessons. Other parents wonder aloud why these skills have to be taught in schools, asking: *Aren't these skills being taught at home anymore?* Other parents feel that this is something that should be their responsibility and do not want any school involvement in this area.

Despite what some may think, SEL isn't new. Teachers have always taught social skills. Yet it seems social emotional learning is everywhere you turn these days. Although the term "SEL" first entered mainstream education around 1994, helping students develop prosocial behaviors has always been a focus in schools. Still, it makes sense that it's in the forefront now. The challenges facing today's students are unparalleled. Constant access to technology, skyrocketing mental health issues, bullying, poverty, drugs, violence, and increased obesity rates plaguing today's youth have been compounded by a global pandemic.

Despite the controversy, research shows that helping students build their social emotional learning skills has many benefits. According to CASEL, it can improve students' academic achievement by 11 percentile points, improve classroom behavior, and reduce stress and depression. And these results have been shown to have long-term (up to 18 years) benefits according to a 2017 meta-analysis.

While those results cost money that schools may be reluctant to spend (social emotional learning curriculum and training isn't free), a study from Columbia University shows that every dollar invested in SEL yields an $11 return.

SEL Programs

The important thing to consider when choosing an SEL program or curriculum is ensuring that it is CURE: Comprehensive, Uniform, Research-based, and Effective. As a result of the pandemic, there has been a rush to implement SEL in schools and there is no shortage of programs from which to choose. Simply selecting a program because the price is right or because it has online asynchronous activities for students learning remotely doesn't mean it will provide the expected results or meet the needs of students and educators over the long term.

- **Comprehensive:** There are hundreds of SEL programs available, with new ones emerging all the time. But many programs offer a singular narrow focus, ranging from mindfulness to yoga. A strong SEL program is one that develops students' skills across all five SEL domains: self-awareness, self-management, relationship skills, decision making, and social awareness.
- **Uniform:** Well-designed SEL programs offer structure and uniformity. They help build a common vocabulary and include developmentally appropriate lessons that are taught in a specific sequence to help teach skills like self-regulation and problem-solving strategies to name a few, so that staff school-wide are on the same page and can repeat and reinforce strategies.
- **Research-based:** Evidence-based research looks at a variety of outcomes for all kinds of students to evaluate the success of SEL programs. Resources such as Blueprints for Healthy Youth Development, CASEL, and What Works Clearinghouse are good places to search for scientifically proven SEL programs. For more on understanding research, see the following page.
- **Effective:** When reviewing research, look for program efficacy. Some SEL programs can improve students' social and academic skills while also improving individual outcomes, creating a positive classroom environment, and improving the school climate overall.

While the global pandemic and other issues facing today's schools have caused many to turn to SEL programming, don't just check the box. Look for high-quality programs that will provide a CURE, which will pay off in the long run.

Understand the Research

When reviewing the research about comprehensive social emotional learning programs, it's important to note that not all research is the same. There's a difference between actual research on a particular program and "research informed" programs. While we won't go into too much detail (such as the difference between a randomized trial versus quasi-experimental or qualitative versus quantitative), here are some questions to consider:

Who conducted the research?
Independent evaluation is important!

Where was the research published?
Peer-reviewed research journals are most reliable.

What did the research measure?
Understand what was being measured, how it is defined, and how they measured it.

What type of research was done?
The quality is in the design; experimental design studies offer the strongest evidence about impact because they show a causal relationship.

What was the sample size?
Size matters, but how the sample was collected is more important. You want to make sure that findings from a sample can be generalized to a larger population.

How many times were the results from the study replicated?
One study is not enough!

Keeping the "Social" in SEL

We understand the realities of trying to teach during a pandemic when schools have a variety of situations to deal with (hybrid, remote, in-person, etc.). When social emotional learning was first introduced in the classroom in the early 1990s, most schools were not tech-savvy, and paper-and-pencil curriculum were de rigueur in the classroom. The pandemic forced many schools to look at remote learning options for their students, including teaching social emotional learning.

While we believe that the best way to teach social emotional skills is still in-person, we know that the needs of our educators and students have had to adapt quickly. Despite this, there is a way to teach social emotional skills without abandoning the social aspects of instruction.

After several decades of research, we also know what works with kids when it comes to teaching SEL skills. For maximum benefit, students should be explicitly taught social emotional learning for a minimum of 20–30 minutes 2–3 times per week, using a high-quality and developmentally appropriate curriculum. So how do we deliver systematic, developmentally based lessons, materials, and instruction to facilitate emotional literacy, self-control, social competence, positive peer relations, and interpersonal problem-solving skills if you can't be face to face?

Here's how!

Get into a Routine

Even in the best of times, kids crave structure and order. During times of uncertainty, sticking to routines can help students to feel less anxious and worried. As much as possible, try to keep your classroom routines intact when teaching remotely. If your week typically starts with a Monday Meeting activity, try to find a way to still have that time together virtually. If you are using an SEL curriculum, try to maintain the routines that they suggest – morning meetings, problem solving meetings, and any other overarching routines that are recommended by the program.

Be Clear and Aim High

We're all still learning how to adapt to remote or hybrid teaching and learning, but that doesn't mean we have to lower our expectations. You know your students best, and you know the kind of work they are capable of. Don't let them take advantage of the situation to turn in work that wouldn't fly if you were in the actual classroom. You can achieve this by making your assignment expectations clear and providing guidelines in simple bullet-point format so that they're easy to understand. Behavior can, and should, be part of those expectations. You can use this opportunity to share a self-regulation strategy or the problem-solving steps with families and encourage students to use the self-regulation strategies at home. This may be especially invaluable to families who are spending a lot of time together in close spaces and are having to negotiate differences!

Prioritize

You may not cover everything you hoped to cover during the school year. That's okay. Decide what is most important and focus on those things. One thing that should be included in your instructional priority list is social emotional learning. Teaching students the specific words to identify the emotions they feel, the understanding that these feelings are okay, and appropriate responses for unpleasant feelings may help students navigate through these uncertain times.

Encourage Connectedness

It's important for students to feel connected even if they can't be physically part of the community. Social emotional learning doesn't occur in isolation, so we need to provide opportunities for students to work together on projects and learn how to be part of a team while working at home. Project-based learning is one way for students to continue to practice these important skills. You can help facilitate that connection by trying to find assignments that students can work on together, such as virtual science fair projects or book clubs. Some of the other grade-level activities include identifying a community service problem to solve together as a classroom. Check out the Buck Institute for Education's PBL Works free resources at: www.pblworks.org/.

Stay in Touch

Social distancing is challenging for everyone, but especially for our students. Create virtual opportunities for students to connect with one another that aren't academic in nature. Your students miss their school, classroom, friends, and their teachers! They want to hear from you. Even if it's just an email to say hi, or specific feedback on an assignment. Those few words mean more to them than you know. So, if you can, take a moment to send that email, or schedule a one-on-one videoconference with your students. Use the opportunity to have an emotion check-in with students. Ask them how they're doing. This can go a long way in helping to keep the social in SEL.

Research shows that to reach the levels of academic achievement that we want for our students, high-quality SEL needs to be at the core of the school curriculum, and that doesn't change just because we are using a new way to impart learning. In traditional school settings, we ask students to turn off their social brain while at school, even though the brain is built to focus on the social world around them. When we teach children using the social and nonsocial parts of the brain, we teach the *whole* child. Learning becomes easier, more enjoyable, and more effective. We have the chance to do that now.

Let's not miss this opportunity!

The Importance of Professional Development

Next to selecting a program to use with students, the most important factor in the success of implementing a social emotional learning program is educating teachers and staff members. A 2019 survey by Education Week Research Center revealed that while nearly 80% of teachers felt that developing SEL skills was part of their job, only 40% felt they had adequate resources to do so. Less than half of all teachers feel their schools provided adequate support for their students' SEL needs. In fact, a 2017 report (the most recent year data is available) by the University of British Columbia for CASEL shows that only six of the 50 states (and District of Columbia) scored high marks for preparing pre-service teachers in three dimensions:

1. Teachers' Social Emotional Learning
2. Students' Social Emotional Learning
3. Learning Context (environments that promote students' SEL skills)

Those states are Connecticut, Hawaii, New Jersey, North Carolina, Rhode Island, and South Carolina. Moreover, in a review of college preparatory programs for teachers in the United States, the "overwhelming majority" of teacher education programs in 49 states do not address any of the five CASEL competencies. Only Utah and the District of Columbia have course requirements that cover one of the five CASEL competencies. Only one university (Widener University in Pennsylvania) in the entire country had a course which addresses all CASEL competencies.

We're glad you're here.

SEL: A Work in Progress

Priti Ahuja knew what she wanted to be when she grew up. "I wanted to be a teacher, but I was socialized to find something else that would make more money. When your family grows up in poverty, they want you to find a job to lift you out of it," she explained.

When she went to college, Priti studied marketing and finance. She started working in a large advertising and marketing firm, got married, and had two children. But she couldn't let go of the teaching dream. "I fell in love with my children. . .and myself," she said.

When the family moved to Chicago, Illinois, Priti took the opportunity to pursue her goal. She enrolled at the Erikson Institute and pursued a Master of Science in Child Development. Next came student teaching. But her big *aha* moment was reading Daniel Goleman's book *Emotional Intelligence*. "It connected with my child development background," she continued. "It changed my life. It was a catalyst."

After teaching in Chicago, the family moved to Dallas, Texas, where Priti continued teaching, but people noticed that she was doing things. . .differently. And they liked it.

Priti built close relationships with her students and their families, had circle time before it was a thing, modeled social emotional learning (SEL) skills, and instead of just teaching an SEL lesson, she and her students practiced it.

"Every week I'd buy flowers. . .and the kids would write a collective note of gratitude to someone and then deliver the note and the flowers. They learned what gratitude looks like, they learned what it feels like. If I had just done a lesson on gratitude and had them write a note once, I'm not sure they would have learned what it is and what it can do for them."

Before long, Priti was promoted to the role of social emotional learning coach, and then started her own coaching business a few years later. "I love my work," Priti said. "There's a lot of professional development. A lot for me to teach and learn."

Priti often starts by building relationships with her colleagues and by encouraging self-compassion and self-care. "I do a lot of research. I stay abreast of what's going on in the field. If I'm telling teachers about self-care, I'm practicing it."

While Priti works hard to stay on top of the latest SEL development, she says it's a work in progress. "There's a lot of noise around SEL right now," she explains. "There's a need to come back to basics. Remembering those foundations and weeding through the noise is really important."

"One thing I wish that everyone knew about SEL is that it's common sense and very simple. If we take away all the formalities, we'd realize that we are doing SEL all the time. . .don't worry about fitting into the competencies. Get back to humanity. Get out of the box." She continued, "I learned at the age of 40 that I had control over my emotions. I can choose not to feel a certain way. Why not teach that to children when they are young? We were all children once. What if we had learned how to live with ourselves and other people? How would that change things?"

CHAPTER 2

Self-Awareness

What Is Self-Awareness?

Before we get started, stop for a moment, and think about self-awareness. What are the top three things that come to mind? Write them down on a piece of paper or in the margin of this book.

When we asked a group of educators to define self-awareness, some of the responses we received were:

> *"Being in tune with your emotions and thoughts, and how they affect the way that you act."*
>
> - Preschool Teacher

> *"The ability to be aware of how and why you are feeling and having skills to solve problems."*
>
> - Elementary School Counselor

> *"Knowing how you are feeling and taking actions to help you be most successful."*
>
> - K–2 Special Education Teacher

> *"The skill of monitoring one's own thoughts/feelings so as to know what an appropriate reaction would be in different situations."*
>
> - 4th Grade Teacher

> *"Open, honest, window view of your feelings and emotions at the moment."*
>
> - Head Start Teacher

> *"Ability to understand your feelings and thoughts and how it influences decisions in my everyday life."*
>
> - Elementary School Teacher

> *"The ability to see yourself through self-reflection."*
>
> - 6th Grade Teacher

How does your list compare?

While none of these definitions of self-awareness are wrong, you can see the wide variety of ideas people have about this domain. CASEL identifies self-awareness as the ability to *"understand one's own emotions, thoughts, and values, and how they influence behavior."* Some guiding questions to build self-awareness are:

- What is my identity?
- What culture(s) do I most identify with?
- What are my core values?
- Do I have a fixed or growth mindset?
- What are my interests and strengths?
- In what areas can I improve?
- What implicit biases, stereotypes, or prejudices do I have?
- What is my purpose?
- How would I rate my level of self-confidence?

Of course, to be self-aware, you have to be able to see yourself objectively, which isn't always easy for young people. It takes time and experience to become self-aware. It also takes the ability to reflect on the past and have introspection to attain greater clarity of self-awareness. These are abilities and skills that are sometimes not even fully developed in adults, never mind young students!

Self-awareness is important. First, it builds a foundation for and is woven through the other four domains of social emotional learning. Specifically, it helps you to:

- **Make decisions**
  When you know your values, you can make decisions that align to those values.
- **Self-manage**
  When you know yourself, it's easier to know what strategies are most helpful when it comes to managing behaviors related to feelings, emotions, or stress.
- **Show social awareness**
  When you value others who are different from you, it's easier to take perspective and have empathy for them.
- **Build relationships**
  When you know your strengths and weaknesses, it's easier to work in collaborative teams with others and show leadership skills.

What Does Current Research Say About Self-Awareness?

There are several issues to address when regarding the research on self-awareness. First is what is "*the self*"? The construction view says that "the self" is really just another concept, like any other concept that the brain uses to make its predictions. You might remember that a concept is our brain's way of making meaning of our experiences and the world. The self-concept might be made up of a number of characteristics such as your likes, dislikes, the roles and responsibilities that you have, the choices you make, your values, morals, and beliefs, your appearance, your cultural identity, and many other characteristics. "A common core runs through all these views: the self is your sense of who you are, and it's continuous through time, as if it were the essence of you." (Feldman Barrett, 190)

Now that you have a sense of the "self," the other thing to note is that the "self" really doesn't exist in isolation. We need other people to help define the "self" because our brain makes predictions by considering our interactions with other people – how they treat us, what they say (or do not say); our actions are dependent on these instances. Our predictions are based on the concepts we have, which are created from our past experiences. So, our interactions with others are necessary to help us define the "self" – the guidelines in which we operate, our dos and don'ts, and our preferences and habits. Essentially, our self-concept is created by a combination of our past experiences, the information from our body (interoception), and the current situation, from which our brain makes its predictions. This includes our interactions with others. Essentially, our self is our past, our present, and our future.

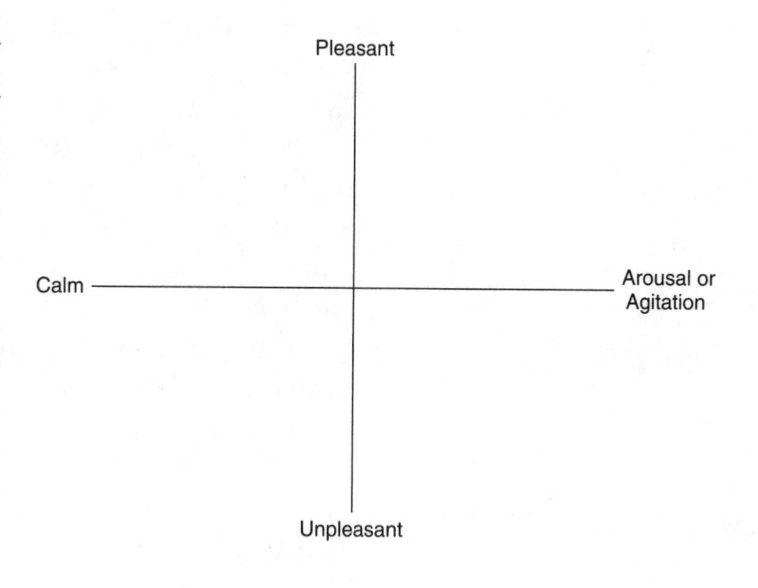

The next thing we need to consider is affect. Affect is our general overall feeling. It comprises feeling pleasant versus unpleasant and calm versus agitated or aroused.

Let's look at some examples of how this chart might work to determine affect. If you were sitting on a park bench enjoying the sun on your face, you might find yourself experiencing a pleasant and calm feeling. If you were driving and someone cut you off, you might feel unpleasantly annoyed. If you were tired because you stayed up too late the night before binge-watching Netflix, you might feel unpleasant but calm. And, if you were at a rock concert, you might feel pleasant and excited. We experience these general overall feelings, which are composed of positive or negative (valence) and active or passive. This occurs based on the interoceptive information, which you might remember is the information that comes from the body and which the brain is perceiving and making appropriate predictions based on this body information.

Affect is determined by the information from our body (interoception), which is constantly being forwarded to our brain for processing. Our brain uses this information from the body (in addition to past and current information) to try to maintain our body budget, also known as allostasis.

Our body budget includes things like:

- Body temperature
- Energy needed to complete the various bodily functions
- Rest
- Hydration
- Maintaining your heartbeat
- Breathing

For example, how much energy will be needed for you to get up and make a sandwich and to get the digestive juices flowing to deal with that sandwich? Or to determine the energy needed for you to get up and put on that sweater because your hands are cold? So, affect is your general overall feeling, based on the information from the body – it's a summary of whether your body budget is balanced or overdrawn – in the black or in the red, so to speak. This information from the body is sent to the brain for processing. Then the brain predicts the body's needs in order to survive, which begins even before birth and continues until death. This means that affect is with us our entire lives and is a fundamental part of who we are and our concept of "self."

Now, affect (our general feeling that is determined by our interoception) can impact how we perceive the world. When you are unsure of the cause of your general overall feeling (affect), you are more likely to attribute the cause to the outside world around you, rather than your internal body information. For example, let's say you get into an argument with a friend, and you determine that they are being both annoying and frustrating. However, you also consider that you haven't eaten lunch today, your glucose levels are low, and you are experiencing stomach pangs. Your friend is being a total jerk, but in truth, you are just really hungry. This is such a shared human feeling/emotion concept, that Merriam-Webster has made it an official word: *hangry*, which is the irritability or anger that stems from hunger. If you've ever experienced an instance of this emotion concept, you will note that as soon as you have something to eat, you feel much better and the person that you thought was a jerk a few minutes ago now seems like such a pleasant person.

Our physical state affects our mental state, which actually means that there is no separation between the two. The interconnection between how we feel in a general way and the state of our body budget is just that – an interconnection. How we feel mentally and how we are doing physically are not two separate things. Given this new information, this holds important implications for the management of our emotional experiences, which we'll discuss in Chapter 3 on self-regulation. It also has some important consequences for our self-awareness. Being aware of our general feeling (active/passive and positive/negative) plays a role in the decisions we make, how we see ourselves and others, and the meanings that we apply to our experiences.

One other thing to consider is our emotion concepts. We perceive emotional experiences because of our emotion concepts. If we do not have a robust conceptual system, our ability to perceive emotion is seriously diminished. The more specificity in emotion concepts that we possess, the more choices we have for predicting, categorizing, and perceiving emotions – we have more options at our disposal so that our brain can predict more effective responses.

"Emotional intelligence (EI) is about getting your brain to construct the most useful instance of the most useful emotion concept in a given situation (and also when not to construct emotions but instances of some other concept). Emotional intelligence is better characterized in terms of concept – the more emotion concepts you have the more options for predicting, categorizing, and perceiving emotion, providing you with the tools for more flexible and functional responses." (Feldman Barrett, 180)

So, to help our brain have more choices, we need to gain more concepts. The easiest way to add to our concepts is to learn new emotion words, because the creation of concepts is strongly linked to language. Each emotion word is connected to that emotion concept that the brain can use to predict instances of emotion. But, if there is no concept, then there is no opportunity to predict that emotional experience. Concepts are like tools in a toolbelt, and if you don't have the tool, you can't use it. So, increasing your emotional vocabulary is like adding tools to your toolbelt.

Emotion granularity is being able to label and define an emotional experience and determine how that experience is different from another similar type of experience. For example, take the difference between disappointed and discouraged. Knowing the definition of these words is helpful but knowing the difference and being able to distinguish between the two using your own experiences is what is important. The differences are subtle but having emotional granularity means having the ability to know how they are different and applying those differences when determining how you feel about a situation. There are approximately 3,000 emotion words in the English language. One study suggests that the average adult uses 15 different emotion words. How many do you know and use on a regular basis?

Another way to increase your emotion concepts is to combine them or create new concepts. As we've mentioned, language is intrinsically linked to the creation of emotion concepts. There are many examples of emotion words in other languages, for which the English language does not have a corresponding word. Therefore, if we don't have the word, our brain doesn't have the ability to predict that instance of emotion – it's lacking the tool (or concept). But we can learn the word and if we use this new word enough, it becomes part of our emotion concepts and can be predicted. Therefore, expanding our vocabulary expands our perceived experiences.

The English language is notorious for borrowing words from other languages (Lomas, 2019). Dr. Tim Lomas' work on lexicography and "untranslatable" words (words that lack an exact equivalent in another language) and wellbeing is an interesting example of helping to create more emotion concepts (Lomas, 2020). He says that words borrowed for cultural reasons are important. These types of culturally borrowed words may "be adopted for pragmatic reasons: it is cognitive and socially useful, allowing speakers to articulate concepts that they had previously struggled to" (Lomas, 6).

Here are some examples of words from other languages, for which English speakers have no equivalent.

Hygge (Danish/Norwegian): a mood of feeling comfortable and cozy, contentment, wellness.
Saudade (Portuguese): sadness or longing for someone who is absent.
Waldeinsamkeit (German): a spiritual feeling of being alone in the forest.
Razbliuto (Russian): a sentimental/nostalgic feeling about someone you once loved.
Jayus (Indonesian): such a poorly told joke that you cannot help but laugh.
Schadenfreude (German): feeling pleasure at someone else's misfortune.

As you can see, from the list, when you read the definition of the word, you may be able to identify with that experience. But not having had the English word meant that it was much more difficult to describe to someone else. As we incorporate new emotion concepts (and as the world community grows), this opens up more opportunities for the brain to predict these instances of emotion.

Similarly, making up new words for an experience and sharing the definition with others and using the unfamiliar words also creates new concepts from which predictions can be made. John Koenig is a master of this, spending nearly seven years writing a dictionary of made-up words. His *The Dictionary of Obscure Sorrows* contains made-up words borrowed from languages all over the world. Some of his made-up words are beginning to enter the English language. He says that he began to make up these words because he wanted to fill the gap and "restore sadness to its original meaning by defining moments of melancholy that we may all feel, but never think to mention – deepening our understanding of each other by broadening the emotional palette. . ." (TED). Here are a few of Koenig's words:

Agnosthesia: *n.* The state of not knowing how you really feel about something.
Lilo: *n.* A friendship that can lie dormant for years, only to pick right back up instantly, as if no time had passed since you last saw each other.
Midding: *v.* feeling the tranquil pleasure of being near a gathering but not quite in it.
Pâro: *n.* the feeling that no matter what you do it is always somehow wrong.

Again, as we read through the definitions, there is something familiar about these described experiences. Using these new words creates new concepts, which helps us to understand our emotional experience more fully.

Now that we've got a better understanding of self-awareness and the constructionists' view, let's see how we can apply this learning to the practice of teaching.

Self-Awareness in Action

Katie S. is a Master Teacher at Educare West DuPage in Illinois, working with children ages six weeks to five years. She uses self-awareness and self-management strategies both in her everyday classroom instruction as well as for her own personal growth.

In the Classroom

"Using an SEL curriculum has really been key to integrating social emotional learning into the classroom," explained Katie. In addition to the curriculum, some of her other favorite ways to help build self-awareness are with a mindfulness program called Calm Classroom, using breathing exercises as well as yoga. These techniques help her and her students tap into their feelings and thoughts, and it complements the SEL curriculum she uses while giving her extra strategies to use as needed. Following each activity, she ensures that students have self-reflection time.

Calm Classroom

"Calm Classroom has been really interesting," says Katie. "We use it two to three times per day. They are short snippets: three-minute activities where the kids are doing mindful breathing or focusing on a bell or shaking their bodies out. Afterward, we reflect on how it made them feel. The reflection piece after these activities is especially important. It gets the kids thinking about how they are feeling and why. We do it when they are calm, so they know to use the strategy when they *aren't* feeling so calm. It helps them to focus on developing some of these important skills."

Diaphragmatic Breathing

Another favorite strategy for self-regulation she uses is diaphragmatic breaths. Katie explains, "Right before nap time, we have them take deep breaths in and out. . .you can feel the energy in the room actually relax." Of course, introducing these new strategies takes patience and practice. "At the beginning of the year, we can only get them to do it for about 30 seconds. But by the end of the year, we are up to 2 to 3 minutes."

Yoga

Katie also does yoga in the classroom. "We start with a short video, or I tell a story. Embedding it in a story makes it work for kids. They incorporate the movement with the story. You can't be too rigid – you have to let them express themselves. It's almost dramatic, pretend play. It's cool to see how they express themselves. I've actually had kids start doing it on their own." Katie details, "They'll be outside, and they'll start acting out a story. It's interesting to see how they use yoga to calm their bodies."

Besides these strategies, Katie uses other tools in her classroom to help with self-awareness and self-management. For example, she tries to anticipate how her students will react and call their attention to it. Katie details, "I'll say something like 'Hey, I notice your body is getting excited. You're moving around a lot. Can you tell me what's going on? How are you feeling?'" Then, she works with them to come up with a plan to deal with what's going on. If the children can't think of their own ideas, she gives them choices. For example, "It seems like you really liked doing ____ before. Is that something you may want to do now?"

For Teachers

When Katie first started her master's program, she was extremely fortunate to have a fantastic mentor. But when she was new to teaching, she didn't always have a mentor and she turned to journal writing. For Katie, the single biggest impact on building her own self-awareness was reflecting.

She explains: "When you're teaching, you aren't being self-aware at that moment. So, every day when I got home,

I would recount what happened and think about how I could improve and reflect. *How am I building relationships with kids? Parents? My team? Why am I here? How am I going to accomplish that?*"

"One day," she explained, "I'd had a really bad day. I had an honest and open moment with myself. I talked to my supervisor. I circled back to the kids. Having a reflective culture encourages those honest conversations. Being honest with kids is super-important. I can say *I made a mistake.* It's good for them to see that even adults make mistakes."

A few other strategies she uses personally are practicing mindfulness, meditation, running, and yoga. "Mindfulness is something that you can do anywhere," Katie says. "Most of us already do mindfulness. We just don't call it that. When you're walking around, and you smell the flowers. When you are focusing on how your body feels today – that's mindfulness. Looking at the sky, relaxing – that's mindfulness. Be intentional about it. It helps you in your practice. You don't have to sit a certain way or put your fingers a certain way."

Self-Awareness Resources: Thermometer Check-ins

Several teachers mentioned the use of SEL thermometer checks for helping students with self-awareness.

The idea is simple: every day, as students enter the classroom, they take a sticky note and indicate how they are feeling at that moment and place it on a large visual thermometer. These emotion check-ins give students the opportunity to identify how they are feeling and teachers the ability to build relationships while simultaneously providing some ideas for appropriate behaviors they can engage in when they feel certain ways. The key for this activity is to ensure students identify how they are feeling at that time as well as strategies they personally find useful.

In addition to the daily thermometer checks as students come into the classroom, teachers can encourage their students to adjust their "temperature" as they notice their feelings change. For students with disabilities and English learners, you can use pictures or color cards to help them describe their feelings. As an added benefit, you can model self-monitoring by doing the activity yourself and telling students out loud when you experience a change in emotion.

There is an example and sample thermometer from the Wisconsin Office of Children's Mental Health (you can download free PDFs in English, Spanish, and Hmong) at: https://children.wi.gov/Pages/FeelingsThermometer.aspx). You can download your preferred PDF version so that students are able to create their own and use it as a reference at home. Encourage parents to engage their children by asking the following questions:

- What's your temperature right now?
- Why do you feel this way?
- How does this make you feel?
- What can you do to feel more comfortable with your emotions?

To help teach self-awareness, you'll also find a sample Feelings Journal in the Resources in the back of this book and SEL lesson plans for self-awareness (and the other four domains) in Chapter 9.

Improve Your Practice

We hope that you've just finished the first chapter thinking, *I WANT to do this in my classroom! I NEED to do this in my classroom.* Well, you CAN do this, and here's how!

Here are three easy practices to build self-awareness in your students (and yourself)!

- **Journaling**
  Encourage students to keep a journal (and keep one yourself, too!) Provide specific prompts to promote self-awareness. Research tells us that focusing on journaling can help with improved adjustment to changes in your life, life satisfaction, and an improved sense of gratitude.

If you're working with younger students, adapt the activity by allowing them to draw their response. Some possible journal prompts include:

- What was one great thing that happened to you today?
- What are you looking forward to?
- What makes you feel calm?
- What goal(s) do you want to reach?
- How do you practice self-care?
- What makes you feel happy? Or sad? Or any other emotion. . .?
- When was the last time you smiled?
- What do you feel grateful for?
- Whom do you look up to? Why?
- What do you do when you're having a bad day?
- What do you wish people knew about you?
- What is your daily routine?
- What is your favorite thing in your room?
- Where do you see yourself in five years?
- What is the best piece of advice you ever received?
- What is your favorite color and why?
- What is your favorite _____ (food, toy, movie, etc.)?
- What are your favorite celebrations, holidays, or other special events?

- **Relaxation Practices**

  Many teachers have discovered the benefits of using yoga, meditation, or mindfulness in the classroom. Of course, these strategies are just one part of a comprehensive SEL program. And remember, these resources don't just help students – they work great for teachers, too! There are a number of free resources available online.

  - **Mindfulness**
    - *Six Seconds: How to Practice Mindfulness for Teachers:* https://www.youtube.com/watch?v=Hb5tM3r4nss
    - Mindful.org: *Best Practices for Bringing Mindfulness into Schools:* https://www.mindful.org/mindfulness-in-education/
    - *Everyday Mindfulness (About Kids Health):* https://www.youtube.com/watch?v=QTsUEOUaWpY

- **Meditation**
  - *20 Terrific Guided Meditations for Teachers (We Are Teachers):* https://www.weareteachers.com/teacher-guided-meditations/
  - *Headspace for Educators:* https://www.headspace.com/educators
  - *Morning Guided Meditation for Teachers (The Mindful Teacher):* http://www.mindfulteacher.com/www.mindfulteacher.com/practice/morning-guided-meditation-teachers.htmlV
- **Yoga**
  - *Kripalu Center for Yoga and Health:* https://kripalu.org/resources/yoga-schools-isn-t-just-kids-how-teachers-benefit
  - *Yoga 4 Classrooms:* http://www.yoga4classrooms.com/yoga-4-classrooms-blog/Teacher-Burnout-yoga-mindfulness-for-teacher-resilience-classroom
  - *Yoga for Teachers/Yoga with Adriene:* https://www.youtube.com/watch?v=zRDQqJEuRcw
- **Vision Boarding**

  Whether it's the beginning, middle, or end of the year, creating vision boards can be a great tool for helping students build self-awareness. At the beginning of the school year, it can help you get to know your students better. If possible, do another at the end of the year, and compare the two. The vision boards you and your students create can be creative and may vary according to your available supplies. There are also a variety of online resources (such as Canva or PicMonkey) that you can use to create digital vision boards.

Reflect on Self-Awareness

In order to help your students improve their social emotional learning skills, you need to develop your own. At the end of each chapter, we'll give you a chance to reflect on the topics we've covered. Please take a moment to spend some time thinking deeply on each of the questions that follow and be honest with yourself in your responses.

What is your reaction to the constructionist view of emotions?

____

____

____

____

How do you model identifying your own emotions in the classroom?

____

____

____

____

How do you recognize your students' strengths and find opportunities to play them up?

____

____

____

____

What would you like to improve in the area of self-awareness?

____

____

____

____

How will you go about improving the area you identified? What immediate steps or actions will you take?

____

____

____

____

CHAPTER 3

Self-Management

What Is Self-Management?

Like most people, you probably think self-management is synonymous with self-control. And based on the responses of other educators, you wouldn't be alone in your thinking:

> *"Self-management is having the self-control to make good decisions for oneself."*
>
> - Occupational Therapist, ages Birth–15

> *"The ability to control one's behavior and emotions appropriately for different settings."*
>
> - K–8 ELL Specialist

> *"Managing your feelings alone and around others."*
>
> - High School Principal

> *"In a word: Resilience. People that are able to bounce back from adversity are able to meet goals."*
>
> - K–12 Teacher Leadership

> *"Being able to react appropriately in a given moment."*
>
> - Elementary Teacher

> *"The ability to regulate one's emotional and physical state."*
>
> - High School Teacher

As with self-awareness, although these responses aren't wrong, self-management is about so much more than just self-control. CASEL identifies self-management as the ability to *"manage one's emotions, thoughts, and behaviors effectively in different situations and to achieve goals and aspirations."*

Some questions one might ask when trying to build self-management are:

- What strategies do you use to manage your emotions?
- What stress management strategies are most effective for you?
- How do you model self-discipline?
- How do you demonstrate self-motivation?
- How do you set and achieve goals?
- What planning and organizational skills are most helpful?
- Are you able to take initiative and ask for help?
- What causes or inspires you to act?

What Does Current Research Say?

If the research on self-awareness seemed challenging, the good news is that the constructionist view of self-management seems much more straightforward. You might remember that the body is sending information to the brain all the time (interoception) and based on that information, the situation/context and your concepts, the brain makes predictions. Sometimes the predictions are instances of emotions.

The basic purpose of the brain is to maintain our body budget – body temperature, heart rate, glucose levels, breathing, hormones, digestion, metabolism – all the systems that keep us alive. If we tried to talk about the connection between the brain, body, and predictions of emotion (or any other prediction the brain might make), it makes it seem that it is possible to separate these ideas into discrete parts. This is not possible, however. The interconnection between these parts is inseparable and as a consequence, this has a significant impact on what we can do to improve self-management. The two most basic ingredients in this process are your body budget and your concepts. And, thankfully, these are two things that you can influence as well. How you choose to do that can either improve your skills of self-management or impact your self-management skills in negative ways.

The first and most basic thing we can do to assist with self-management is to focus on our body budget and the things that influence its working well – sleep, proper nutrition, and exercise.

Sleep

Sleep is especially important to allow your body to recharge, and many experts agree that most adults need between seven and nine hours per night according to the Centers for Disease Control and Prevention. An internal clock, which lets us know when we feel tired or alert, operates on a 24-hour cycle, known as circadian rhythm. Our circadian rhythm can be influenced by chemicals in the brain and our exposure to either natural or artificial light. Both these influences help the brain to figure out whether it is time to wake up or time to go to sleep.

Once we are asleep, there are four stages that last from about 90 to 120 minutes a cycle. The first stage is 1 non-rapid eye movement (NREM) and this is the period of light sleep, where breathing, heart rate, eye movement, brain waves slow down, and muscles relax. The second stage is 2 NREM where things slow down even more and body temperature decreases. This stage is typically the longest in the sleep cycle. During stage 3 NREM is where the deepest sleep occurs, muscles relax, and blood pressure and breathing drops. Finally, during stage 4, REM occurs, which stands for rapid eye movement. Dreaming can occur during this stage.

All this is interesting, but why is sleep so important to us as educators? There is quite a bit of scientific evidence today to indicate that a lack of sleep has a direct impact on cognitive ability and school performance. This is concerning because a lack of sleep can have a direct impact on mental processes such as attention, memory, slow reaction time, and the ability to absorb and analyze information. It can impair sequential thinking (following a set of instructions) and creative thinking skills. There are also significant effects on mood and behavior such as daytime drowsiness, poor decision-making, aggression, irritability or moodiness, hyperactivity and/or depression, and anxiety. When taken altogether, a lack of sleep is a significant barrier to effective teaching and learning.

There are a number of causes attributed to a lack of sleep, such as inconsistent sleep schedules, sleep as a low priority, electronics use at bedtime, sleep disorders, or other health concerns. So, what can schools do about students suffering from a lack of sleep? When you know better, you do better. So, let's educate our students (and their parents) on the importance of sleep, what can happen when you don't get enough sleep (how it affects you mentally and physically and the subsequent impact that it can have on academic performance), and what they can try to do about it.

1. Prioritize getting a good night's sleep.
2. Set a consistent bedtime.
3. Create a relaxing bedtime routine.
4. Stop using technology about one hour before bedtime and remove devices in the bedroom to avoid temptation.
5. Make your bed as cozy as possible.
6. If there are still sleep issues, consult a health professional.

A sleep journal can be a helpful tool to provide insight into sleep patterns and identify what might be getting in the way of a good night's sleep. Information that should be kept in a sleep journal are:

- What time did you go to bed?
- How long did it take you to fall asleep?
- When did you wake up in the morning?
- How often did you wake up during the night?
- What caused you to wake up during the night?
- Do you feel refreshed in the morning?
- Do you drink any caffeinated beverages? If so, how many during the day?
- Are you taking any medications that might affect your sleep?
- Are you getting enough exercise?
- Did you stick to your relaxing bedtime routine?
- What time did you stop using a screen?

Having discussions with students about the importance of sleep can be helpful in drawing awareness to this issue. Encouraging students to use a sleep journal and discussing the results of the journal in the classroom can bring awareness to the connection between lack of sleep and academic performance.

Nutrition

Proper nutrition is also important and impacts our overall feeling or affect (see Chapter 2 to remind yourself about affect). So, what is proper nutrition or a balanced diet? The US Department of Health and Human Services has an entire guideline that you can download or order at https://health.gov/our-work/food-nutrition/previous-dietary-guidelines/2015. But, if that seems too daunting, here's a brief overview of their five guidelines.

1. Healthy eating is for your whole life, not just a short period of time. Healthy eating patterns include an appropriate calorie level for both achieving and maintaining a healthy body weight to reduce the risk of disease. The average adult requires approximately 2,000 calories per day to maintain their bodyweight but this is also dependent upon age, sex, and level of activity.

Person	**Calorie requirements**
Sedentary children: 2–8 years	1,000–1,400
Active children: 2–8 years	1,000–2,000
Females: 9–13 years	1,400–2,200
Males: 9–13 years	1,600–2,600
Active females: 14–30 years	2,400
Sedentary females: 14–30 years	1,800–2,000
Active males: 14–30 years	2,800–3,200
Sedentary males: 14–30 years	2,000–2,600
Active people: 30 years and over	2,000–3,000
Sedentary people: 30 years and over	1,600–2,400

2. Nourish your body with a variety of food choices from all food groups in proper amounts. A balanced diet includes fresh fruits and vegetables, whole grains, legumes, nuts and seeds, and lean proteins.
3. Limit sugar, saturated fats, and sodium.
4. Choose foods and beverages that are healthier choices.
5. Healthy eating is for everyone.

A balanced diet provides your body with the ingredients it needs to work properly. When a body does not get enough nutrients, it is at risk of developing disease and poor performance. It's like when you put regular gas into a sports car. Eventually, it damages your engine, and it doesn't run as efficiently. There are significant scientific studies that now link poor diet to disease such as heart disease, cancer, stroke, and Type 2 diabetes. It is a challenge in our busy lives to ensure a healthy diet. When you consider that it affects not only your body's health, but also your overall feeling of well-being, choosing to eat an apple over a bag of chips might just make the difference between feeling good that day and feeling blah.

So, what can schools do to promote healthy eating? Many schools today offer a breakfast program and/or free/reduced lunches, and often school social activities include meals or snacks. If that's the case at your school, encourage those in charge of these programs to ensure healthy food options for students. The Centers for Disease Control and Prevention have a lot to say on the subject, encouraging schools to *"play an important role in shaping lifelong healthy eating habits through federal child nutrition programs."* They also encourage schools to communicate with families about proper nutrition. They have four suggestions for schools looking to ensure healthy eating among their student body:

1. Provide breakfast at school.
2. Ensure enough time to eat lunch.
3. Promote healthy eating throughout the day.
4. Include nutritional education as part of academic instruction.

You may even want to consider starting a school/community garden. Research shows that schools can play a key role in students' health. According to research from Columbia University, students in schools that provide frequent, high-quality opportunities for hands-on nutrition learning eat up to three times more fruits and vegetables at school lunch. More importantly, those benefits extended to children's home eating habits as well. The USDA has some advice for how to start your own school garden: https://www.usda.gov/media/blog/2013/08/13/start-school-garden-heres-how/.

Families living in poverty face numerous challenges, but one significant challenge is trying to provide nutritious meals that include all the food groups. Providing fresh fruits and vegetables is particularly challenging and often outside the meal budget or difficult to come by at food banks. Although there are nutritionists that insist a healthy, balanced diet can be achieved on most budgets, the reality is often the food choices that are made on a low budget do not achieve these lofty goals. The choice of tasty, cheap, and convenient foods often wins out over foods that require more preparation, effort, and cost. Canned, dried, and prepackaged foods also spoil less and last longer in the family cupboard. The response for many schools is to offer meals – breakfast and lunch – for their students. There are numerous federal and state programs that provide funding and assistance because the connection between student academic success and proper nutrition is clear. Food is the fuel for the body and brain and proper nutrition is the difference between success and failure on so many levels.

Exercise

The third thing that you can do to help maintain your body budget is to get up off the couch and become more active. If you love to read scientific articles, there are a plethora of choices on why you should exercise. The benefits of exercise range from increasing energy, controlling weight, and improving overall health, mood, and sleep. And again, the U.S. Department of Health and Human Services has some recommendations.

1. Get at least 150 minutes of moderate aerobic activity spread over the week – so get out, walk, and enjoy the stroll through your neighborhood or park, choose to walk short distances rather than hop in the car, take your dog for a walk, take the stairs rather than the elevator. Every little bit helps and adds up over the week.
2. Try some strength training exercises – strong muscles build strong bones, and as we age our independence is contingent on flexibility and strength. A person who was an inspiration in this area was Justice Ruth Bader Ginsburg. Her fitness routine was legendary, and she maintained her twice-a-week workouts well into her 80s.

An important part of nutrition is exercise. According to the CDC, childhood obesity is a genuine problem in the US, with nearly 20% of children affected with obesity, which affects children at all grade levels and can lead to serious health problems. Getting active can help not just with reducing obesity, but also to help students feel, function, and sleep better. Being active for most children means about 60 minutes of physical activity daily. This includes going for a walk, biking, or playing soccer.

You may remember that the brain makes predictions based on interoception, the current situation, and its concepts. How does this predictive brain react to a body that is unhealthy? It is slow to respond to errors, and over time we can begin to feel chronically unwell. So, to keep your body budget balanced, attend to the basics of proper sleep, nutrition, and exercise.

Working with Your Concepts

The second thing you can do is to work with your concepts. As adults, we have choices in what and how we expose ourselves to experiences. These experiences impact our learning and ultimately our concepts (from which our brain makes predictions). So, the choices we make today impact our concepts tomorrow, which may change the predictions that our brains make. The following are some effective strategies that impact our concepts.

Deconstruction

Deconstruction is learning to identify the physical sensations that you are experiencing in that moment. When you are experiencing an emotional response that is difficult for you, taking stock of the physical sensations is a first step in learning how to recategorize your experiences. Have you ever experienced sweaty palms, a flushed face, or a racing heartbeat at the same time that you are expected to stand up in front of an audience and give a speech? Rather than think that you are experiencing anxiety, could these same physical sensations also indicate enthusiasm, excitement, or anticipation? What if you noticed that you were experiencing sensations of discomfort in your stomach, that you felt jittery, and that you were having difficulty focusing on a task and all this was occurring about lunchtime and you had a dentist appointment that afternoon? Could it be that you were worried about the dentist appointment, or might it be that you were just hungry? Breaking our physical sensations down into their parts and looking at the causes from a unique perspective is the first step in the strategy of recategorizing.

Recategorization

Recategorization and improved emotional granularity go hand in hand. The more concepts you know and instances you can construct, the more well-developed concepts you have to choose from to recategorize an experience. Recategorizing helps you to regulate your behavior in more useful ways. We can attempt to transform how we perceive the physical sensations from something that is difficult or challenging to deal with, into something that is more pleasurable but at the same time, challenging.

There are significant benefits to recategorizing such as improved academic performance and greater stamina when you categorize discomfort as helpful. When we recategorize discomfort as helpful, we can perceive this discomfort as the body managing the experience. When we view the experience as manageable, despite it being challenging, this promotes a more "can do" perspective. Let's give it a try.

Anxiety could transform into anticipation.
Nervousness into determination.

Worry into ________________________________.

Fear into ________________________________.

There is solid evidence to suggest that recategorizing works to impact your concepts and potentially affect your brain's predictive nature.

Rumination has negative effects. When you perseverate on an issue, it's as if you are experiencing that negative experience over and over again. You can see how this might significantly affect your concept formation and potentially increase the chances of your brain predicting an instance of emotion in an event that might be similar in the future. The more well-developed the concept the greater the chance of prediction. Rather than spending time rehashing the negative situation, the time is far better spent on thinking about what you can learn from the experience and how to constructively deal with similar situations in the future.

Emotional Granularity

We also discussed improving emotional granularity in Chapter 2 on self-awareness, but how can improved emotional granularity help us with self-management? When we have a greater understanding of our emotions and an ability to distinguish the subtle differences between emotional experiences, this offers greater choice and flexibility on our brains' predictions – more well-defined concepts, more choice of predictions. Therefore, learning new words for emotional experiences and being able to identify them in our daily lives helps change the predictions our brains make. Quickly review this chapter's introduction on how to improve your emotional granularity.

Gratitude

Gratitude, giving and keeping track of positive experiences through journaling, or other creative means can also impact our concepts. By focusing on things that we perceive as positive, we can add to our concepts in ways that bolster and build them with attention to the good things in our lives. Studies link positivity to improved immune function and increased health benefits, reduced anxiety, work performance, and greater happiness. There are numerous research studies that focus on positivity, gratitude, and giving, and a new area of psychology has emerged within the last several decades. Positive psychology focuses on several key ideas like seeking out pleasurable experiences, engaging fully in things that you enjoy, looking for meaningful experiences outside of yourself, expressing gratitude, savoring pleasurable experiences, being mindful (present and non-judgmental), and having self-compassion. All of which help to enhance our more pleasurable concepts and increase our chances of more positive instances of emotion predictions.

Social Reality

Using agreed-upon concepts, or social reality, by creating tools to help us deal with difficult circumstances can be especially helpful in learning to master your emotional experiences and learning how to calm down. Inventing and sharing concepts that can be used as tools for challenging situations can be incredibly helpful! Many programs offer structures for calming down, problem solving, and goal setting. Teaching these structures in our schools, modeling their use, and encouraging students to use them during difficult times works. Universal self-regulation strategies and routines have seen incredible success for students in the area of self-management. Schools see a decrease in volatility in classrooms, fewer detentions and suspensions, and an increased ability to manage strong unpleasant emotional situations among children from preschool and upward.

Self-Management in Action

Since most teachers we spoke to were focused on self-regulation when it comes to self-management, the ideas in this section focus on that area as well. However, please check out the Goal Setting lesson in Chapter 9 for another example of self-management in action.

In the Classroom

In the Emozi middle school SEL program, we use the SCOPE Strategy to help students with self-regulation. SCOPE stands for:

1. **S**top and take some deep breaths.
2. **C**onsider how we are feeling and why.
3. **O**ptions – what can we do?
4. **P**lan – what are the steps?
5. **E**valuate the outcome.

In the Resources section, you'll find a poster you can use to remind your students about the SCOPE Strategy as well as keep track of other self-regulation strategies that work best for them.

Some other ideas for encouraging self-management in the classroom:

- Work with students to develop classroom protocols. Provide a review as needed so students know expectations and how to manage their own behaviors.
- Set learning goals and meet with students periodically to review their progress toward those goals.
- Encourage students (and model yourself) to identify how they feel and why. This will help students in two ways: It helps them identify specific feelings/emotions and recognize behaviors that are appropriate for the feeling.

Let's look at an example. It's the block just before recess. It's finally a nice day outside, and while you're trying to teach a science lesson, you can tell the students are excited to get outside to play. There are a few possible reactions to this situation:

1. "Why isn't anyone listening or paying attention to this lesson? I am going to have to keep you inside for recess if we don't get through all this, so focus!"
2. "Wow, I can see that you are all excited to go to recess. I am excited, too. But we still have 15 minutes left in class and a little more information to cover. When I'm feeling excited, sometimes it helps me to focus if I get up and stretch, so how about if we all stand up and take a one-minute movement break and then finish up this lesson."

In the first example, the educator has not recognized or acknowledged how the students might be feeling. The students are left to wonder what the appropriate response is for feeling excited. In the second example, three things have happened: The teacher has both recognized and acknowledged how the students feel and given an appropriate behavior suggestion. While it might seem like these types of interactions will create more interruptions in the classroom, you'll find that the exact opposite is true, and over time you will have fewer interruptions.

Finally, it's important to note that there are many things that can interfere with a student's ability to self-regulate. Examples provided by educators we've spoken with include abuse, learning disabilities, trauma, distraction, maturity, and not being explicitly taught. These approaches to help students build their self-management skills take time and practice, so have patience with the process.

For Teachers

When it comes to self-management for teachers, self-care is key! According to research from the National Education Association, 40–50% of new teachers leave the profession in the first year. The ones who stay report feeling demoralized and burned out. And this was before a global pandemic threw education into a tailspin. The following seven skills will help lower your stress and keep your sanity.

1. **Learn to say no**
   We get it. Teachers are expected to be superheroes. But sometimes you just have to say no. Covering for someone during your prep time? Sorry. Someone trying to pull you into a last-minute meeting? Nope. Set boundaries and stick to them. And while you don't have to give an excuse or reason for not doing it, learn to say: *I have plans.* Repeat after us: *I'd love to, but I have plans.*
2. **Prioritize**
   There are times when you simply cannot say no. When this happens, prioritize. If you have a problem deciding what's most important, ask! *I'd love to attend the last-minute meeting, but is it more important than completing progress reports today?*

3. **Nap (Yes, really!)**
   Research shows that the average adult doesn't get enough sleep. Teachers are no exception. You'll be a better teacher, parent, and person if you get enough sleep. If that isn't possible, consider a quick nap. Just 10–20 minutes is a long enough power nap to rejuvenate you. Anything less is not enough and anything more than 30 minutes can actually make you groggy, a state called "sleep inertia."
4. **Rest**
   If you can't take a power nap, consider a brief rest. Sometimes referred to as "quiet wakefulness," resting can be much less stressful than napping because you're not trying so hard to sleep and you can do it anywhere! Just find a comfy spot, set a timer, and close your eyes. The National Sleep Foundation reports that resting has almost as many positive benefits as napping, so go for it!
5. **Meditation**
   Meditation is not the same as resting or napping. When we rest, we are simply closing our eyes and recharging. Meditation is similar, but you remain alert to your surroundings. Meditation is another great strategy to help you relax and reduce stress. If you're interested, there are a ton of free apps available. Check out the list in the online resources at http://www.wiley.com/go/socialemotionalclassroom.
6. **Exercise**
   We all know the benefits of exercise and working out, but who has the time? There are plenty of ways to sneak some exercise into your busy school day.
   - Park your car as far away from the front door as you can.
   - Take the stairs instead of the elevator.
   - Bring sneakers and walk the track (or around the building) during lunch or before/after school.
   - Make exercise part of your classroom instruction. Think: yoga, movement minutes, etc.
   - Stuck at your desk? Try sitting leg lifts or arm curls.
7. **Do something you love**
   Some folks think that taking time for yourself is a luxury. But giving yourself time to do the things you love, whether it's hanging out with a friend, reading, or another hobby, will help you feel better. When you feel better, you can be the best version of yourself.

   Don't be afraid to try several different techniques for self-care. It can take some time and practice to find what works best for you.

10 Questions with a Teacher: Integrating SEL in Unconventional Ways

Name: Katie B.

Subject/Grades Taught: Veteran highly qualified teacher, currently teaching STEAM and enrichment in a rural elementary school in New Hampshire.

---

1. **Why do you think it is important to teach Social Emotional Learning?**
   In education we talk all the time about making sure our students are "college and career ready." To me, the skills covered in SEL, especially the CASEL competencies, are the most critical skills students need to be college and career ready, or really just "life ready." We are in the business of preparing kids for their future, whatever that may look like, and SEL skills are the foundation for a successful and fulfilling future.

2. **Was SEL part of your pre-service training?**
   Not officially, but I feel like it fell under the umbrella of classroom management. It wasn't really a thing. In grad school, we didn't talk about SEL in any official way.

3. **Have you ever had any formal training in SEL?**
   Yes, I feel like it's most of what we do now. Our district adopted the *No Bully* program a few years ago, and we all got trained, but then it sort of disappeared. We are a PBIS school in theory, so a lot of what we do is focused on SEL, even if it's not a particular program. We also have an SEL consultant who comes in, and each building gets a few hours each year. They are focused on SEL practices and improving school climate.

4. **Has the district made SEL a priority?**
   Very much so. Our last PD day was devoted to SEL and teacher self-care. In the last six to seven years, it's increasingly become a priority. And we've always had guidance counselors pushing into the classroom with SEL lessons and activities.

5. **Do you have the resources (materials, training, etc.) you need to teach SEL effectively?**
   I feel like I was always effective with SEL – before it had a name. When we named it and we started focusing on it, I lost some of the natural practices that I had woven

(*continued*)

into my classroom. When we started being told we had to do this many minutes and this many lessons, I felt like it became less natural and less successful for me. For me, I lost what felt natural.

When I first started teaching, I felt like I built students' SEL through literature, studying texts, building classroom communities, and being a responsible classroom. I got the job done with basic principles and high-quality themes and texts. My classes were cohesive little communities that took care of each other and advocated for each other. Parents were engaged and involved. Then something changed. And I don't know what happened. It became less authentic. I've had this conversation a lot with colleagues. We thought, *Yeah, we do this. It's built into teachable moments. We don't need to sit down and have formal class lessons about it.* We need it to be authentic and based on what we'd do naturally in the classroom. There are teachers who really need these types of lessons, but SEL comes naturally to me. There has to be room for both.

6. **Can you give us an example?**
I have a set list of texts that we read every year. I chose them because they have messages that become a foundation for our classroom and how we treat each other. One of those is *Mr. Peabody's Apples* by Madonna. It has an important lesson about self-management and social responsibility. . .The kids got it, and all year long we referred to it.
I tell the students how when I first saw it was a book by Madonna, I dismissed it. I had a preconceived notion of who she was, and then I read it and was like, *Oh wow!* I was totally judging. Sharing with kids our own vulnerability is important. I had to be willing to say to the kids, *I did it too.* If we want to be successful with SEL, we gotta be real. We can't come at them from on high.

7. **What SEL domains (self-awareness, social awareness, decision making, relationship skills, self-management) or skills do you think are MOST important for students to master in order to be successful in life?**
Self-management and responsible decision-making are the two that are most important. When you're dysregulated, it's almost like the hierarchy of needs – none of the other things can happen. You don't have the mental space available to do the other things and navigate

(*continued*)

those challenges if you're not regulated. And decision making because if you make decisions that put you in bad situations, or make decisions that are bad, you won't be able to do anything else.

8. **What do your students think about SEL?**
   I think they know about SEL now because we are much more intentional about it, but I'm not sure they call it SEL. They'd probably call it "mindfulness" or the "guidance counselor lesson." They would recognize that it's not academic. But without a lesson like *Mr. Peabody's Apples,* they would not have realized it's anything but a reading lesson.
   For kids at this age, it's easier to see things in other people than themselves. It's easier to talk about things that others are involved in. It takes some of the pressure off, and they talk about the situation and strategies, and it lets them be more open.
9. **How has parenting impacted the way you teach SEL?**
   Actually, my parenting has been informed by my knowledge of SEL. There are so many situations that should be easy because I'm a teacher. But I've come to realize that most things involving kids are not as easy as I would have thought. I do get told (by my children) that I'm talking to them like a student. It's perplexing when something doesn't work, I think: *This worked in the classroom. It's in the textbook. Why isn't it working at home?*
10. **What's one thing you wish everyone knew about SEL?**
    I wish that teachers knew that they're probably already doing it but they don't realize it. There isn't one way to do it. It looks different in every classroom. And don't be afraid to be vulnerable with your students (in an appropriate way) and make connections with them.

Improve Your Practice

Here are three easy practices to build self-management in your students (and yourself)!

- Balance the Body Budget
  Keeping your body healthy can impact the way you feel. Speak to your doctor for specific details about how to best care for yourself or you can follow the general guidelines below.

Nutrition: The US Department of Agriculture (https://www.myplate.gov/) has a quiz you can take to help you determine how healthy you are eating. There's also a dietary guideline booklet, and a free app to help you track healthy food choices, recipes and more!

Sleep: According to the Centers for Disease Control, the average adult needs 7–9 hours of sleep per night. Their tips for getting a better night's sleep include having a consistent schedule, turning off all electronics before bedtime, ensuring your room is calm and relaxing, avoiding food or drinks before bedtime, and ensuring you get some exercise every day.

Exercise: The American Heart Association recommends that adults get at least 2.5 hours of moderate physical activity per week. You can visit their website for additional information, ideas, and tips for ways to achieve that goal: https://www.heart.org/en/healthy-living/fitness/fitness-basics/aha-recs-for-physical-activity-in-adults.

Water: Everyone knows how important water is, but most of us don't drink enough in a day. The National Academies of Science, Engineering, and Medicine suggests that a healthy adult should consume 4–6 cups per day.

Keep Track of Your Body Budget Account

There are a number of native, free, or low-cost apps you can use to track your food, water intake, exercise, and sleep, or you can use the log below to keep track.

Sample Body Budget Log

	Sleep Goal: ______	Nutrition Goal: ______	Exercise Goal: ______	Water Goal: ______	Goal: ______
Monday					
Tuesday					
Wednesday					
Thursday					
Friday					
Saturday					
Sunday					
Monday					
Tuesday					
Wednesday					
Thursday					
Friday					
Saturday					
Sunday					

- **Mandalas and Zentangles**
  A mandala is a symbol made up of geometric patterns and organic forms. It can have a spiritual meaning for some, but it's also sometimes used to help people focus or meditate. A sample mandala is below. There are a number of free online tutorial videos that illustrate how to make a mandala, or you can find directions here: www.wikihow.com/Draw-a-Mandala.

Similar to a mandala, a zentangle is a mindful doodle composed of recurring patterns and shapes. View the sample below. There are a number of online tutorial videos that illustrate how to make a zentangle, or you can find directions here: https://zentangle.com/pages/get-started.

Reflect on Self-Management

Please spend some time thinking deeply on each of the following questions. There are no right or wrong answers, but please be honest with yourself in your responses.

What would you like to improve in the area of self-management?

How will you go about improving the area you identified? What immediate steps or actions will you take?

What are some healthy strategies you use when trying to self-regulate?

Are there any unhealthy ways you self-regulate that you'd like to eliminate from your life?

CHAPTER 4

Social Awareness

What Is Social Awareness?

Of all the CASEL domains, social awareness was the most misunderstood by those we interviewed. When we asked a group of educators to define social awareness, their responses varied. Given the redefining of the competency in 2020 by CASEL, it's easy to understand why. Here's what educators had to say about social awareness:

> *"Being aware of our own identity and how you respond to it and knowing that others come from different backgrounds, cultures and contexts, and having an openness, appreciation and understanding for others."*
> - Coach for Teachers in PK–8

> *"Knowing how you are feeling and why."*
> - K–2 Teacher

> *"It's bringing everyone at a level of understanding how we connect with each other and learning from each other."*
> - Social Worker in an Alternative Education Setting

> *"Being able to empathize with others and see things from multiple perspectives."*
> - 4th/5th Grade Teacher

CASEL identifies social awareness as the ability to "understand the perspectives of and empathize with others, including those from diverse backgrounds, cultures, and contexts."

Some people refer to social awareness simply as diversity; however, it's much more than that. Some questions one might ask when trying to understand social awareness are:

- In what ways do you consider the perspective of people from different backgrounds and cultures?
- What social and ethical norms do you recognize and follow?

- Are there social norms in your community that you feel are unjust?
- What supports are available to you in your school and community?
- How do you recognize strengths in others? How do you recognize your own?
- How do you demonstrate empathy and compassion to others?
- In what ways do you express gratitude? And how often?
- What is your understanding of how organizations and systems influence behavior?

What Does Current Research Say?

There are basically two important points to know about social awareness and current research:

1. We cannot "read" how other people feel by merely observing their facial expressions and body language.
2. The body budget, or allostasis, is really at the root of socialization and the need for relationships.

These two statements might be different from what you were taught, so, let's take a closer look at them and what the research says.

Reading Between the Laugh Lines

Most of us may assume that when someone is happy, they typically smile. When someone is feeling sad, they might have a frown, or cry. When someone is feeling mad, they might yell. This belief is commonly held in society and we often accept it as fact. . .but in reality, it is just one understanding, and it is inaccurate. Let's explain.

Take an example of a wedding. Typically, a wedding is often a joyous experience. You might see people laughing, smiling, dancing, crying. . .wait! Crying? Yes, we've seen some people cry at very happy occasions. Are we to conclude that because they are crying, they are not happy? No. Happy people cry sometimes.

These are some examples of experiences of emotion that are predicted by the brain, yet the responses do not fit into the culturally assumed categories. If we were relying upon facial expression or body language, we might make inaccurate assumptions about how others are feeling. For us to be more accurate in our perceptions of other people's emotions, we must accept that we cannot always accurately "read" other people. Our perceptions of other people's emotions are only guesses and these guesses are based on our concepts.

However, there are times that it might feel that you can accurately predict other people's emotions from time to time. If that is so, how does this happen? The reason that we are able to guess what someone else is thinking or feeling is because our concept of the situation matches closely with the other person's concept of the situation.

Who Doesn't Love a Surprise Party?

Let's say that you have a friend for whom you plan a surprise party. In this scenario, you love surprises and would be thrilled if someone planned a surprise party for you. Your concept of a good surprise includes surprise parties. If your friend also has a similar concept of good surprises, which also includes surprise parties, your prediction that they will love a surprise party makes sense. However, a problem occurs if the two of you have quite different concepts of surprises.

Many of us have found ourselves in situations where someone thinks we're going to be extremely happy with the situation, but in fact we find ourselves feeling exactly the opposite of our friend's expectations. This is due to the fact that our concepts are not aligned. Dr. Barrett says, "Emotional communication happens, therefore, when you and I predict and categorize in synchrony." (Feldman Barrett, p. 195)

As you may recall, our emotions are a result of predictions. We can observe our interactions with another person. These interactions either confirm our predictions or become prediction errors. When this happens, our brains can either make new predictions or ignore the contrary evidence. These new predictions represent learning and can help us to create alignment with other people, improving our social awareness. If our brains ignore the contrary evidence and we do not change our interactions, we do not create alignment. This results in misreading social situations.

Let's go back to the surprise party that you've thrown for your friend. You see your friend enter the party. They smile and laugh and immediately move into the room to greet the party guests. Based on this information, you might interpret that your friend is pleased with the party and loves surprise parties as much as you do. But many of us have had experiences where we need to pretend to be enjoying a situation that actually brings us tremendous discomfort. Our success in deceiving those around us depends upon how good we are at acting and/or whether those around us ignore our behaviors that might indicate that, to the contrary, we are not having the time of our lives.

This may seem complicated, and you might wonder how we manage to connect with others effectively. Sharing cultural backgrounds or past experiences helps us to have more similar concepts from which predictions can be made. If we also agree on the meaning of certain facial expressions, body language, and ways we communicate in certain situations, that is also helpful. Over time, we can collaborate and create an emotional experience that we both can identify with – these concepts that we've co-created don't have to be exact, just close enough to have a similar meaning for both of us. By co-constructing our experiences, we regulate each other's body budgets.

How Our Relationships Impact Body Budget

This brings us to point number two concerning socialization, relationships, and the effect of allostasis (body budget). How do our relationships impact our body budget? In the 2018 article "Growing a social brain" in the journal *Nature Human Behaviour*, the authors hypothesized that allostasis or body budget regulation is dependent upon socialization and the individual's physiology for survival. This article discusses parental care and infant body budgeting which provides optimal circumstances for brain development and learning. They suggest that socialization is an acquired skill which emerges from the nurturing and body budgeting regulation process, which begins with the parent/child relationship. They provide examples of mothers feeding, singing to, and touching their infants, which helps to regulate temperature, heart rate, sleep, etc.

This caregiver relationship is the first social competency to be mastered. The caregiver relationship is seen as highly rewarding (from an allostasis/body budget perspective), promotes infant attachment to the caregiver, and thus motivates them toward social interactions. "According to our framework, social animals are not born with a predetermined "social brain," but rather biologically adapt to become social as a result of allostasis dependency." (Atzil, W., et al p 625) This regulation of the body budget between mother and infant promotes learned synchrony. These actions by mothers promote body budget regulation in the baby, which is one of the first social competencies of infants.

The next social competency to master is joint attention. This is where the baby learns to attend with mother/caregiver in a shared experience. This usually begins to occur around six months of age. Once this occurs, the caregiver can begin to direct learning toward important social and cultural information through talking, looking, and touching. An example of joint attention might be the mother pointing to a stuffed animal and saying the name of the animal and the baby looking toward the object to which their mother is pointing. Joint attention allows infants to gain the knowledge needed to survive in their environment.

Thus, the human brain is a social brain, whose development is initiated by the need for allostasis regulation, influenced by the caregiver relationship and developed through ongoing social interactions. The relationship between one brain and another is profound and forms a system that "sustains many of our human features including knowledge, skill and biology." (Atzil, W., et al p 632)

At the end of the day, we are taught to be social beings, who have learned that our body budget regulation and shared understanding of concepts is intricately tied to others. And with that, there are a few things we can do to improve our social-awareness skills. Since we cannot read each other with accuracy, we must accept that our interpretations of how others are perceiving the world are not facts. We have to take the responsibility to ask how other people are experiencing the situation and rely upon their responses, rather than our flawed interpretations. On the other hand, we also have to take the responsibility to ensure that we are being clear in our communication. If we want others to predict effectively and for them to sync with our concepts, we have to be good communicators.

Think Before You Speak/Words Matter

The other important thing to remember is that words matter and that we can influence others' predictions by the words we choose. How do we want them to perceive the situation? Do our words match up with our intentions? For example, if we want our partner to express how they are feeling about a situation, choosing to ask, "How are you feeling about the situation?" might be better than, "Are you upset about the situation?" The first question allows for any emotional response to be communicated and the second question narrows the playing field to just whether they're upset or not. It also might indicate that the situation should be upsetting, and so their response should indicate that they are, in fact, upset. Words matter. Choose wisely.

Social Awareness in Action: A Case Study on the Power of High Expectations

When she first became a teacher 15 years ago, Amy* taught in a district that took part in a program called *Accept the Challenge*. Students who were admitted to the program their first year of high school were provided with mentors who coached them on how to have high academic achievement. If they successfully participated in the program for all four years, they'd get a four-year scholarship to a local college when they graduated from high school.

To provide a bit of context, it's helpful to understand a little bit about where Amy taught. Lawrence is an urban city located on the Merrimack River in Massachusetts. According to the 2020 Census, Lawrence is home to just under 90,000 residents. It was also the site for one of the first union strikes in the country – the Bread and Roses Strike – which was organized in 1912 to protest substandard conditions and pay cuts to the largely immigrant workforce in the city's abundant textile mills.

In 2019, the median household income in Lawrence was $44,613 – almost half the average for the rest of the state. Just over 80% of the people living in Lawrence self-identify as Hispanic, and half of that number were born outside of the US. Over half of the population (67%) has a high school diploma and 10% have at least a bachelor's degree.

As a first-year high school English teacher, Amy started the school year full of energy and excitement, determined to make a difference. With her syllabus and culturally relevant book list in hand, she set up her welcoming classroom and embraced all her students. But what she learned during student teaching was not her reality. "Many of my students were reading way below the 9th grade reading level. I didn't have books for them to read. Many of my students were newcomers or English learners, so I spent most of my time developing basic literacy skills and teaching basic grammar, which I really wasn't trained to do," she explained.

---

*To protect teacher and students' privacy, real names were not used in this article.

Still, when she found out about the *Accept the Challenge* program, she identified some students in her classes who she thought had potential. "Of the 100-plus students I saw on a given day, I could select only one from each class period to participate in the program." In hindsight, she recognizes that her criteria for inclusion in the program was somewhat arbitrary:

- Who consistently did homework?
- Who worked hard and participated in class?
- Who was "smart"?
- Which students had families that would provide the support they needed to be successful?

Based on these criteria, Amy selected five students. They were accepted into the program and participated for their entire high school career. Now, 15 years later, she's proud of their accomplishments, which include:

Javier: Got his BS degree in public health and now works for an organization to improve engagement for Hispanic communities on health-related issues.

Gabriela: Got her undergraduate degree in education. While working as a preschool teacher, she attended graduate school, earning a degree in mental health. She now works in the community as a counselor.

Jaime: Got his undergraduate degree in criminology and is working as a corrections officer.

Isabella: After working toward her undergraduate degree in human development and psychology, she studied abroad and then went on to get a Master's in Education with a concentration in counseling. Today, she's a counselor at the very same high school she attended!

Marianna: After earning her undergraduate degree in marketing, she went on to get a master's degree in business and now works for a global company.

Of course, this doesn't mean none of Amy's other students were successful. There were certainly other success stories. For example, Mateo owns an auto body shop. "He drives a nicer car than I do!" Amy says. Miguel has a successful barber shop. Sofía is a social media beauty influencer. Maria works in healthcare.

While Amy is immensely proud of all her students, she says, "In hindsight, it's somewhat disheartening to think of how the outcomes could have been different for all of my students if I had identified each one of them as having potential and enrolling them as program participants. What if I had the same high expectations for all of them or thought they all possessed the criteria to be successful? This bothers me to this day."

In the Classroom

For Teachers

Showing empathy, expressing gratitude, and perspective taking were identified as an almost three-way tie by educators as the most important social awareness skills that students need to be successful in life.

To help bolster those skills, a teacher from Canada uses the 7 Sacred Teachings (https://empoweringthespirit.ca/) with her students to help build their social awareness, especially around issues that impact First Nation communities. She also encourages students to bring in artifacts from home and invites families into the classroom to share their cultures and traditions with the class.

There are other ways to incorporate social awareness into your classroom. Some teachers role-play situations in which they have students take different points of view, play charades, or present *What Would You Do?* scenarios.

Another activity some teachers mentioned was doing talk circles. Doing the talking circle builds communication, trust, confidence, pride of who they are, and they begin to connect with themselves and others. Another teaches students to talk and write about current events and tie them to their social studies lessons.

One way to help bolster social awareness is to encourage students to look at an issue from a different perspective. Try using the prompts on the following page. (You can download this resource from the book's web page, http://www.wiley.com/go/socialemotionalclassroom.) You can use this when discussing themes from a work of literature or a historical event. It could also be used to form the foundation of a debate – you could even have students complete the form and then ask them to present another student's perspective.

Resources

Understanding Perspective

My point of view is:

____

____

The opposing point of view is:

____

____

This perspective is based on:

____

____

Evidence to support this:

____

____

How does this influence the perspective?

____

____

This is different from my perspective because:

____

____

Improve Your Practice

Here are three easy practices to build social awareness in your students (and yourself)! Showing gratitude, identifying community supports, and taking part in community service projects are a few ways to improve social awareness.

Keep a Gratitude Journal

There's quite a bit of research about gratitude and the role it plays in shaping social awareness. In one study by Dr. Robert Emmons of the University of California, Davis, and Dr. Michael McCullough of the University of Miami, participants were asked to write a few sentences each week, focusing on specific topics. One group was asked to write about things they were grateful for that had occurred during the week. The second group was asked to write about daily irritations. Finally, a third group was asked to write about events that had affected them (with no emphasis on whether they were positive or negative).

After ten weeks, those in the first group (who wrote about gratitude) were more optimistic and felt better about their lives. They also exercised more and had fewer visits to physicians than those in the other two groups.

Another leading researcher, Dr. Martin Seligman, from the University of Pennsylvania, found that when someone wrote and personally delivered a letter of gratitude to someone who had never been properly thanked for their kindness, they exhibited a huge increase in their level of happiness. This impact was demonstrated to last for a month!

A synthesis of research from Positive Psychology on gratitude has shown other benefits of gratitude. Gratitude has been found to improve sleep, self-esteem, and relationships. Physical and psychological health also saw benefits of gratitude.

Research from the Youth Gratitude Project shows that "when compared with their less grateful peers, grateful youth are happier and more satisfied with their lives, friends, family, neighborhood, and selves. They also report more hope, engagement with their hobbies, higher GPAs, and less envy, depression, and materialism."

One easy way to show gratitude is by keeping a journal. Of course, you can purchase a fancy gratitude journal, or you can just record one or two simple statements of gratitude in a notebook, or use the THnx4 online gratitude journal: https://ggsc.berkeley.edu/what_we_do/online_courses_tools/thnx4_gratitude_journal.

For inspiration, check out Ross Gay's essays, *The Book of Delights*, in which the author wrote about something delightful every day for a year.

After her husband suddenly passed away, Sheryl Sandberg, the COO of Facebook, wrote a book called Option B Facing Adversity, Building Resilience, and Finding Joy with Adam Grant. In it, they detail how you can face adversity and build resilience to find joy in everyday life. In a commencement speech she delivered at UC Berkeley, she said, "Finding gratitude and appreciation is key to resilience. People who take the time to list things they are grateful for are happier and healthier. It turns out that counting your blessings can actually increase your blessings. My New Year's resolution this year is to write down three moments of joy before I go to bed each night. This simple practice has changed my life.

Because no matter what happens each day, I go to sleep thinking of something cheerful. Try it."

Start small. Little things count, too. Some examples:

- The first crocus peeking out in early spring.
- Your child performing well on a project or assignment.
- The sound of a bird chirping.
- Getting the perfect cup of coffee/tea/cocoa.
- Mastering a skill you've been working on.
- Making (or eating) your favorite meal.
- Getting a good night's sleep.
- Talking to an old friend.
- Reading a good book.
- Hearing your favorite song.
- Taking your pet for a walk.
- Sunshine!
- Random acts of kindness.

Gratitude Journal Sample

January 8
Morning: Grateful for the person who bought my coffee this morning at the drive-thru!
Evening: Kids loaded the dishwasher without complaining. Yay! Progress.

March 20
Today is the first day of spring. I am grateful for the beautiful weather. The sun feels great after a long and cold winter. I'm even grateful that the kids are antsy. It brings excitement and energy into the classroom.

April 17
Three things I'm grateful for today:

1. Coffee!
2. I made it to work on time.
3. Sun is shining.

June 11
Grateful that another school year is over. Proud of all the achievements my students have made this year. Grateful for the ability to sleep in and not worry about lesson planning!!!

September 4
Looking forward to meeting my new class and grateful for the chance to reconnect with colleagues. Also, grateful my own kids are back to school! Bonus: Gratitude that they've learned to make their own lunches!

November 24
I'm grateful that all my friends and family are healthy and safe this year. I'm looking forward to safely celebrating the holidays with my family.

Research Community Supports

An important part of social awareness is knowing what supports are available in your community. These are supports that can help you or your students.

Of course, the types of support that are available will vary depending on where you live. But in general, there are five types of support that may be available in your community:

1. **School**
   Examples include: School counselor, health services, free/reduced lunch, etc. Lebron James' *I* Promise school (https://ipromise.school/) has even provided bikes and Taco Tuesday dinners for their families.
2. **Local (City/Town)**
   Check with local community service organizations to see what kind of options are available. Some examples include libraries, food pantry, clothing drives, medical/dental services, etc.
3. **State**
   Your state may have a number of options for those who need them, such as services for individuals with disabilities or those without healthcare. Examples include transition services, resources for the visually or hearing impaired.
4. **National**
   Depending on where you live, there may be federal resources available, such as those for anti-bullying, substance abuse, or suicide prevention.
5. **Nonprofit Organizations**
   There are many nonprofits that seek to help educators and students. Examples include mentoring organizations (MENTOR) and volunteer organizations (Volunteer Match or Do Something), to name a few.

Complete Community Service Projects

Community service comes in many forms, and the best part is – not only does it help the community, it can help increase self-confidence, decrease depression, and can even help you to be physically healthier while strengthening your relationships with others!

If you're looking for community service ideas and aren't sure where to start, check out these options:

www.dosomething.org/us; www.volunteermatch.org/; https://engage.pointsoflight.org/. If you're still struggling to find a way to become connected to the community, try asking yourself these questions:

- What issues are you and your students concerned about?
- What causes do you care about?
- What kinds of activities do you enjoy?
- What special skills or services can you provide to an organization?
- What are your gifts and strengths/talents?
- What are the specific needs in your community?

Adapt and Adjust: A Pragmatic SEL Implementation in Indiana

When you speak to Dr. Danny Lackey, his first career as a mental health counselor shines through, despite the fact that he's been in education for almost three decades – as a middle school guidance counselor, diversity coordinator, and now as the executive director of student support services at a medium-sized school district in Indiana.

Because of this background, in his district, social emotional learning (SEL) was an important focus before the pandemic and will continue to be long after. He said, "If there's a silver lining to the pandemic, it's that it helped teachers have an increasing understanding of the value of SEL. . .there was more communication with teachers, families, and students. Families also gained empathy for what teachers go through."

Dr. Lackey first approached SEL through the lens of mental health three years ago. He explained, "When we began looking at student health and wellbeing, it came out of our social work department. In the data we collected, we saw an uptick in the area of ACES [Adverse Childhood Experiences] and the alarms went off for us."

"You can't expect teachers to facilitate curriculum if they aren't taken care of. . . and cannot make the assumption every teacher understands what SEL is and why it's important."

But they didn't wait until it became a crisis situation. They decided to be proactive and start addressing the problems right away. Still, Dr. Lackey knew that the solution wouldn't be immediate and obvious. "As an administrator, we like things wrapped up in a bow, all planned out. . .It doesn't work that way. I had to navigate my role with the expectations and reality of how things are. We took it step by step and sometimes had to stop and reevaluate and modify to keep it going."

They began by forming an SEL committee to look at how to address SEL at each school for students and teachers. "Our rationale was that you can't expect teachers to facilitate curriculum if they aren't taken care of. . .and you cannot make the assumption that every teacher understands what SEL is and why it's important," he explained.

As next steps, the district selected and piloted an SEL curriculum and training for teachers. But Dr. Lackey explained, "The biggest hurdle was that some saw it as a burden – another thing on their plate. What I neglected to look at was I didn't fully think through how it impacts the systems of the teachers. You need the buy-in of the teachers to be able to implement it."

For the next several months, they had conversations with teachers. Some hard truths came out of those meetings, and not every meeting ended successfully. "We pulled out student data and showed them," said Lackey, "and they got it pretty quickly. Buy-in is the most important piece. Teachers have to think: *I can see how that would benefit my kids and make it easier to teach my kids.* If you don't answer the question of, *Why are we doing this?* you will never get fidelity of implementation."

Another important part of any effective SEL implementation is the support of the building level administrator. "That process always included building level admin. It is key. An admin can tell you what's on the teachers' plate. They have to be the voice. They have to show their support." Getting support from school counselors, social workers, school support staff, paraprofessionals, and even the teachers' union would also be essential for the success of their SEL program.

> ***"Buy-in is the most important piece. Teachers have to think: I can see how that would benefit my kids and make it easier to teach my kids."***

Instead of a mandatory one-size-fits-all approach to implementing SEL in the district, they pivoted, and created district level standards with freedom of choice for each building in meeting those expectations. Lackey reasoned, "We all have to be on the same page on what needs to happen as a district, and it may look a little different in each building. Each building has its own culture. Each admin is different. The teaching staff is different. Every building has different priorities. I am okay with that. Because you are not going to move the needle in an authentic way if you do not accept where people are at. The needle will move superficially; the move will be temporary."

They also began looking more closely at the social emotional needs of the teachers. "Our teachers are exhausted," he said. "They need time to recover. But we wanted to give them an opportunity. It's important to give teachers choices." Some of the unique ways the district is helping the social emotional health of their educators is by providing ongoing optional workshops and training (and time to do them as well as compensation for attending), creating a mindfulness room, bringing in a Tai Chi instructor, facilitating study circles, initiating conversations on race and systemic racism, and creating a calendar with an SEL focus of the month. "We wanted to make sure teachers feel like they have the support and resources to deliver the SEL curriculum confidently. We need to invest in our teachers. Continue to show them how they are already meeting SEL competencies. Show them how to integrate SEL into the curriculum they teach every day and how they can integrate it naturally."

After a full year of this transitional approach, there have been success stories. Some schools have implemented the SEL curriculum for the entire year. Some are still working on it, but the fact that most teachers are implementing some SEL activities in their daily routines is a plus. Perhaps the most positive outcome for Dr. Lackey is, "Teachers are being more mindful and aware of the students. They know about the unfortunate stressors our kids are experiencing, and they take them more seriously in the conversations they have with the kids."

Based on past experience, Dr. Lackey knows he'll have to be a bit more fluid next year with their SEL implementation. While there are expectations and standards, it could change. "When we get back together next year, we'll ask: Is the plan viable? Do we need to change? There is comfort in operating in that way."

Reflect on Social Awareness

Please take a moment to spend some time thinking deeply on each of the social awareness reflection questions and be honest with yourself in your responses.

Do you have high expectations for your students? For yourself? Explain.

How does your perspective influence the way you teach?

What are some ways that you show gratitude in your daily life?

Name some community resources that could be helpful or community service projects you'd like to be involved in.

CHAPTER 5

Relationship Skills

What Are Relationship Skills?

Asking what relationship skills are might seem like a rhetorical question. Let's take a look at some of the responses we received from educators:

> *"The ability to be authentic, communicate well, repair relational injuries, suspend judgment, and create zest and the desire for more contact (see Jean Baker Miller's work)."*
>
> - Professional Development Instructor

> *"Effective communication and the ability to recognize and adapt to different situations."*
>
> - Elementary Homeschooler

> *"The ability to interact with others in a positive, healthy manner that allows both/all parties to be comfortable and feel included."*
>
> - 1st Grade Teacher

The relationship skills domain is a little tricky, because although it's about relationships, it also touches on all the other competencies. CASEL identifies relationships skills as the ability to *"establish and maintain healthy and supportive relationships and to effectively navigate settings with diverse individuals and groups."*

Simply put, relationships skills are your ability to connect with others. Some questions one might ask when trying to understand relationships skills are:

- What is my ability to establish and maintain relationships with people who are different from me?
- How do I communicate effectively and clearly?
- Do I cooperate well with others, including practicing teamwork and collaboration?
- What is my ability to resist inappropriate social pressure?

- How do I negotiate conflict constructively?
- Do I seek and offer help when needed?
- How do I demonstrate cultural competency?
- In what ways do I show leadership and problem-solve?
- How comfortable am I standing up for the rights of others?

What Does Current Research Say?

Social awareness skills are the skills necessary to help us interact more effectively. The latest research has much to say on this topic. But, first, let us remind ourselves about one important fact: Our brain is social, not because we were born that way, but because of the caregiver/infant relationship and the need for allostasis (body budgeting). The caregiver/infant relationship teaches the brain that this social connection is helpful to maintain allostasis. In Chapter 4, we learned that the caregiver/infant relationship helps the infant's brain to regulate the body budget and predict bodily requirements. Through this relationship, the infant learns that the brain's need for allostasis can be met via this social connection and thus the social brain is created – we learn that our relationship with others can help regulate our body budget.

So, the brain learns to be a social brain, and it also needs a map of how it views the world. This is so that it can interact with others and use this map or mental model of the world to begin to make predictions. This mental model helps us navigate through the social landscape. As an infant, this map is formed and as we understand more about the world and our relationship to it, we add or make adjustments. Once we have a foundation, the brain uses this as a guide to make predictions. Remember that the brain uses its predictive process to be metabolically efficient. When the brain accurately predicts, it is less costly. However, when errors occur, we need to alter our model of the world – this is learning, and it comes at a metabolic cost. In the short term, we expend energy to build a mental model from which accurate predictions about the world can be based. In the long term, we can minimize this metabolic cost and become more efficient; short-term pain for long-term gain. We learn to invest wisely, balancing between improving our mental model of the world and conserving metabolic energy.

Relationships then, are really about two things: our behavior and others' expectations of our behavior. If we behave differently from what others expect, we are less predictable and more metabolically costly to others. As we learn about relationships, there are two developmental tasks that are necessary. First, we learn to accurately predict others' behaviors in response to our actions. This starts with the caregiver/infant relationship as stated previously. As the infant's mental model of the world becomes more sophisticated, the infant's predictions become more accurate, decreasing the metabolic cost associated with prediction error. But for the infant to build a useful mental model, prediction error is high, and there is substantial learning that needs to occur. As we learn to act in more predictable ways, we decrease the metabolic cost to us and to others.

The second developmental task is to understand what is socially required of us. As we get better at predicting social norms, the relationship between how we behave and what is expected is clarified. We are able to anticipate how people will respond when we behave as expected and how they will respond when we don't. These two developmental tasks, accurately predicting others' behaviors and understanding how our behaviors influence others' responses, are foundational to our understanding of relationships.

Learning about others can be metabolically costly. When we do what others are expecting us to do, they in turn will hopefully do what we expect of them. When others behave in ways we do not anticipate, we experience prediction errors. For us to mitigate this metabolic cost, we can conform to the expectations of others, so that they will likely react as expected.

Imagine you have been invited to a birthday party for a friend. You receive an invitation, and it requests that you RSVP by a certain date. You conform to the expectation by responding during the timeframe that you will attend the party. When you show up at the party, the expectation is that the host will act in a friendly and cordial manner. If, however, you do not respond to the invitation and just show up at the party, you may feel unsure about how you will be received. This lack of surety is a metabolic cost to you.

We become better at this by having experiences that teach us what is expected and how others will likely behave. As children develop, have more social experiences, and are directly taught what is expected of them, their ability to negotiate their social world improves. There is a high metabolic cost to this learning curve, but as they gain more skill and experience, the metabolic cost decreases.

We can reduce our prediction error by participating in social groups that have similar beliefs, behaviors, and ways of communicating. This is called social cohesion. The more we interact with a group, the easier it becomes to understand each other. This shared experience helps us to clarify expectations of each other. Therefore, by following what is expected, we can minimize the potential randomness of their actions and behavior. This minimizes the metabolic cost to all concerned.

So, if having information about how we should behave is helpful to us, how helpful would it be if we were deliberately taught some of these skills, rather than by trial and error? How helpful would that be to our predictions? How helpful might it be metabolically? By explicitly teaching relationship skills such as collaboration, problem solving, motivation, friendship, and communication skills, we help move the learning process forward exponentially. If we are intentionally taught these skills, we can reduce the metabolic cost that occurs when our brain predicts incorrectly. Rather than trial and error, if we are taught these skills intentionally, we can learn what is expected and begin to practice and hone our skills, maximizing the effort and time expended/invested.

Programs that teach relationship skills to students are proven to be highly effective. The metabolic benefits of reducing prediction errors are advantageous if children are exposed to these sorts of experiences when they are young. The benefits also exist as we age, because relationship skills are not something that we only learn as a child. As we mature, we build upon our relationship skills inventory. For example, when we are little, we learn that others think differently. When we are a bit older, we add onto this understanding by seeking mutually beneficial solutions to problems. This leads to the ability to skillfully negotiate more complex problems and develop leadership skills. We can decrease the metabolic cost by teaching these skills and promote lifelong learning.

Relationship Skills in Action

In our interviews with educators, teachers overwhelmingly felt that some of the most important skills for successful relationship skills are communication, problem-solving, and self-advocacy.

There are a number of well-known, researched, and evidence-based problem-solving and conflict resolution strategies and programs used in classrooms today. For example, Positive Behavioral Interventions and Supports (PBIS) and the Good Behavior Game. For the purpose of this chapter, we focus on the two biggest challenges that teachers say their students face: resolving conflicts with peers and family members and building healthy teacher-student relationships.

In the Classroom

Remember that in many cases, students spend more time at school than they do at home. That means that teachers often play a vital role in developing the social emotional skills of students. The relationships that students build with their teachers are important. In addition to parental influence, the teacher/student relationship can often be the model that young children use to form healthy relationships with other adults as well as with their peers. In addition, teachers help build students' self-confidence, which often reduces behavioral problems in the classroom, and results in high levels of school engagement and academic achievement.

According to What Works Clearinghouse, here are some things you can do to build relationships with students at all grade levels:

Elementary School

- Engage in one-to-one interactions when possible.
- Get down to the child's level during face-to-face interactions.
- Use a pleasant, calm voice and make eye contact.
- Provide appropriate responsive physical contact.
- Follow the child's lead and interest during play.
- Help children understand classroom expectations.
- Redirect children when they become challenging.
- Listen to children and encourage them to listen to others.
- Acknowledge accomplishments and efforts as well as individual strengths.

Middle and High School

- Think about each students' individual needs.
- Greet and welcome students at the door of your classroom at the start of each period.
- Recognize students' cultural and linguistic gifts.
- Encourage students to pursue their interests.
- Give them space and time when they need and be available.
- Model vulnerability so they feel safe doing the same.
- Encourage students to communicate.
- Encourage students to try to resolve their conflicts and differences and offer support.

Improve Your Practice

Here are some additional strategies to encourage the use of relationships skills in the classroom.

- **Build Connections**
  Research shows that SEL is most effective when it is coordinated within the community and integrated at home with students' families. Families, schools, and communities all impact students' learning, development, and experiences. Inequities based on race, ethnicity, class, language, gender identity, sexual orientation, disability, and other factors impact students. While SEL alone will not cure these problems, it can create the conditions needed for individuals and schools to create more equitable and inclusive learning environments that encourage the interests and assets of all individuals.
  Look for ways to include the community into your classroom. When students see you value your classroom community, they will, too.
- **Understand Communication Styles**
  There are four basic communication styles: Passive, Aggressive, Assertive, and Passive-Aggressive. Understanding the traits of each and how you (and others) prefer to communicate can help improve your relationships.

Communication Style	What It Looks Like	What It Sounds Like	How to Work with Others with the Style
Aggressive	Demanding and dominating; often poor listeners who refuse to give in, aggressive body language	Yelling, demands others; *"You can't do anything right."*	You may be tempted to react by yelling back but try pausing before responding to calm down. *"I can see that this might not be the best time to discuss __, so let's wait until later."*
Assertive	The ideal communication style, good listener, open, fair, confident	Calm and considerate; *"I hear what you're saying but have you considered the other point of view?"*	Ensure that you are also sharing your viewpoint and being listened to. *"You're a good listener, but I want to make sure you really understand. . ."*
Passive	Avoids conflict, gives in, lets others make decisions	Timid and shy; *"Sure, whatever, it doesn't matter to me."*	Validate the person's feelings to try to get to the heart of the issue. *"I know it must be frustrating, but. . ."*

(continued)

Communication Style	What It Looks Like	What It Sounds Like	How to Work with Others with the Style
Passive-Aggressive	Frustration and discomfort; can't communicate how they really feel	Sarcastic, resentful, and oppositional. *"I'd* love *to help. . ."*	Model the conversation, *"What I'm hearing you say is ___, but I'm confused about what you mean."*

- **Encourage Teamwork and Collaboration**
  Use this list of Collaborative Working Group Norms as a guideline when developing your own rules to encourage students to work cooperatively.

Collaborative Working Group Norms

PK/K
- Use inside voices
- Don't interrupt
- Be kind
- Listen

Grades 1–3
- Listen to the person speaking
- Don't interrupt
- Make eye contact
- Be kind and honest

Grades 4–6
- Listen to the person speaking
- Don't interrupt
- Be kind and honest
- Be respectful
- Explain your reasoning
- Use "I" Statements

Grades 7–8
- Listen to the person speaking
- Don't interrupt
- Ask questions
- Be respectful
- Explain your reasoning
- Use "I" Statements

Grades 9–12
- Listen to the person speaking
- Don't interrupt
- Consider all viewpoints
- Be respectful
- Explain your reasoning
- Ask probing questions

Reflect on Relationship Skills

Please take a moment to spend some time thinking deeply on each of the questions below and be honest with yourself in your responses.

What are some ways that you build connections and relationships with your students?

How do you communicate best?

What would you like to improve in the area of relationship skills?

How will you go about improving the area you identified? What immediate steps or actions will you take?

SEL: It's Not More on Your Plate, It *Is* the Plate

Ann McGreevy is the Supervisor of Mental Health and Psychological Services for the Frederick County Public Schools (FCPS) in Frederick, Maryland. But she never thought she'd end up working in education. "I had no idea what I wanted to do in college," Ann continued. "I liked psychology and majored in clinical psychology, but there wasn't much I could do with that."

After graduating, Ann took a contracting job for FCPS, working in Psychological Services completing psychological evaluations for special education eligibility before she was offered an opportunity as a school psychologist. It was an offer she couldn't refuse. She explains, "I loved being a school psychologist. I did that for 10 years and then was promoted to the role I have now."

Things have changed a lot over the past three decades that Ann has worked in education, but one thing that hasn't changed is her commitment to social emotional learning (SEL). "I did not get any SEL training as part of my undergraduate or graduate coursework to be a clinical psychologist. We got training in a lot of the same underlying competencies, but it wasn't called SEL. I've been doing my own research for six or seven years. I was part of an FCPS work group that researched SEL and evidence-based SEL Curricula. We started looking at CASEL and research behind SEL in general."

She continued, "SEL exploded about six years ago. People began to understand what it is and why it's important. Also, there was less of a stigma around mental health. We have a better understanding of trauma and adverse childhood experiences (ACE) and what it does to a child's brain. It's just as important to teach SEL as it is an academic subject. It doesn't matter how much you know about something if you can't get along with people or regulate your emotions. SEL is a developmental set of skills and competencies that need to be taught in order for a person to gain them. They, like other acquired learning, need to be directly taught and practiced. We aren't born with these competencies."

Getting to the point where everyone understood Ann's vision and agreed on the importance of SEL was not an overnight success story. Some of the things that have helped change many people's mindsets around SEL and mental health in general include the increased presence of social media, technology, bullying, a recession, the pandemic, and the opioid epidemic. "Back in the day, more families were teaching SEL as part of parenting. Some students came to school with many basic SEL skills, and some did not," Ann detailed. "SEL helps level the playing field for all students. For many kids, they come to preschool and kindergarten, and they have the appropriate SEL skills. But some kids come to school, and they don't have them; yet we have specific behavioral expectations for them when they come to school."

Still, integrating SEL was a process that took some time. "In our county, we had principals asking for help," she continued, "So I asked, what if we invest in social emotional learning for every child so there is less need for individual staff such as psychologists and behavioral specialists? Fortunately, our superintendent saw the benefits of this, and we presented it to the board of educa-

(*continued*)

tion, and they understood the significance immediately. We identified grant funding, so it didn't cost the school system a dime in the budget. It's hard to argue with that. Everyone at the leadership level bought in. Everyone agreed."

Ann knew that getting buy-in from teachers was crucial for the program to succeed, and the superintendent was explicit with her support and set the expectation. Explicit SEL instruction was mandatory for all students in FCPS up through Grade 8 (and optional but highly suggested for high school), and all teachers and staff members were trained on how to implement the SEL curriculum. Ann recalled the superintendent's response: "She said that SEL isn't one more thing on their plate. SEL is the plate." They have 30 minutes twice a week to teach SEL during any content area. All schools have periods for SEL built into their schedule.

Already, SEL is becoming part of the culture at FCPS, and it's just as important as academics. "If you spend 20 minutes or so teaching this, you will save just as many minutes correcting behaviors. Students will be available to learn. You'll have far fewer interruptions. Back in the day we did not teach all the names and definitions of emotions. We didn't talk about feelings as much. It's so much easier for a child to say they're frustrated and need help versus feeling frustrated and throwing stuff. Now they know the words. If there's one thing I wish that everyone knew about SEL, it's that it is developmental, that it can be taught, and that it must be taught if we want kids to be successful!"

Timeline of SEL Implementation

2018–2019 School Year
FCPS held a workgroup exploring SEL and available curricula. The team included four elementary school principals, two school psychologists, and the coordinator of behavioral supports.

2019–2020 School Year
Field testing of three different programs in four different elementary schools and data collection.

Summer 2020
Curriculum selected and purchased using funding from a Safe Schools grant.

2020–2021 School Year
Curriculum rolled out in every elementary school for Grades PK–2. Mandatory usage twice a week for 30 minutes each.

2021–2022 School Year
Curriculum rolled out in every elementary school for Grades 3–5. Mandatory usage twice a week for 30 minutes. Virtual SEL curriculum purchased for all middle and high schools (mandatory usage in the middle school only).

2021–2022 School Year
A middle school SEL curriculum was purchased, and all teachers were trained. Every middle school in the county is teaching the same SEL curriculum twice a week.

High Schools have a large bank of SEL resources for teachers to pick from organized by the 5 SEL competencies. Three high schools will field test a SEL curriculum.

CHAPTER 6

Responsible Decision Making

What Is Responsible Decision Making?

As with relationship skills, asking educators to define responsible decision making may seem rhetorical. But we asked anyway and ended up getting the best description we've seen of any competency:

> *"Decision making is the process of coming to a final verdict between two or more possible choices. It is taking into account the pros, cons, and possible outcomes of each step that you make in your lifelong journey."*

CASEL identifies decision making as the ability to *"make caring and constructive choices about personal behavior and social interactions across diverse situations."*

Simply put, responsible decision making is your ability to consider all variables when making decisions using problem-solving skills. Some questions one might ask when practicing responsible decision making are:

- What criteria do you use to make ethical choices?
- How do your behavior and your social interactions align with social norms?
- Do you consider the consequences of your actions?
- Do you demonstrate curiosity and open-mindedness?
- When making decisions, do you tend to analyze information, data, and facts or just go with your gut?
- How do you identify solutions for problems?
- Do you use critical thinking skills?
- What is your role in ensuring personal, family, and community well-being?
- How do your decisions impact the community?

What Does Current Research Say?

There are many reasons as to why we evolved from a single-celled organism to a multicellular organism, but a key attribute is predictive regulation.

Our brain gathers information from inside the body and outside the body from the environment. It uses this information and weighs the risks and rewards and then makes its predictions based on its concepts and on what will serve the best interest. It chooses the appropriate actions and metabolic requirements needed to support the prediction because prediction is a more efficient method than waiting for errors to occur and then trying to correct them again and again.

As you may recall, learning occurs when there is a prediction error. Prediction error is costly, metabolically speaking, because the brain has directed resources that were not needed or provided resources that were insufficient to the task. If you are sitting in a chair and decide to get up, but you don't push the chair back far enough, you bang your knee against the leg of the table. Your brain predicted how much energy was needed for you to push the chair back and then recruited the necessary energy for you to stand up. However, bashing your knee against the leg of the table really hurts and that prediction error might result in a bruise. Your brain learns that it's got to recruit more energy to push the chair even farther back than it thought was initially necessary, the next time you find yourself sitting in the chair and need to get up. So, by remembering experiences, we learn what we should repeat and what we should not.

The brain also learns from experiences that produce better than hoped for results. When this happens, we get a little hit of a chemical called dopamine. Dopamine is a reward for the brain, providing a brief uplift to your affect and helping to encourage the brain to remember the experience and hopefully repeat it. An example of this might be starting a conversation at the lunch table with someone new. You get a hit of dopamine upon finding out that they have similar interests; the result is a pleasant conversation. The dopamine helps the brain remember the positive interaction, increasing the likelihood that you will start a conversation with a stranger in the future. The next conversation you have with a stranger might not always lead to a pleasant conversation, but the possibility now exists in your concepts.

Over hundreds of thousands of years, our brain developed into a complex organ with its sole purpose to maintain allostasis (body budget). It is a predicting brain that learns through prediction error, adding to its concepts, creating a mental model/map of the world, and is encouraged to remember things, in part, by small hits of dopamine (among other things). So, what gives us this hit of dopamine? In the past, when we were hunters and gatherers, it would have been small things such as coming across a bush particularly rich in berries, finding some herbs that we might need for medicinal purposes, or finding a hare that we have caught in a snare. It also might be the comradery of spending time around a campfire, painting pottery, singing songs, or sharing stories. These encounters require that we are fairly proficient in the skills that keep us alive as well as a creative outlet for sharing these experiences. They require our full engagement with both mind and body.

We are also social beings, which we learn how to be as infants through the caregiver/infant relationship. This helps to regulate many of the infant's physical needs. Our brain's sole purpose is to maintain allostasis, so we learn to be social because of this physical regulation. We learn that our relationships with others can help regulate our bodies. When we're having a good time with friends, we can feel better emotionally and physically. When we're in an argument with someone, we can feel emotionally and physically sick.

So, how does all this link back to self-regulation and decision making? In part, it has to do with our body budget and what you can do to make an impact like getting proper sleep, eating well, and exercising. These are things that you can work with, which affects the information the body sends to the brain, which impacts predictions. See Chapter 3 for more specifics on the body's requirements and what you can do to improve your overall health. When information from the body is optimal, this affects your brain's predictions. For example, if you've had a good night's sleep, you wake up feeling rested and energized. If you have things that are challenging or difficult that day, you are more likely to face them in a more positive frame of mind. Contrast that same scenario with when you've had a horrible night's sleep and a challenging day. Your perspective on whether or not you can deal with these challenges might be less than optimal. Making decisions that impact your health in positive ways is the most basic way to affect your predictions and therefore your self-regulation and decision making.

Two other ideas help us to understand improved decision making and problem solving. The first is the theory of social construction, and the second is developing our concepts of problem solving. Let's look at each one.

The Theory of Social Construction

The Theory of Social Construction relies on two points: that reality is a social construction, and that language is the primary way we communicate that reality. As was mentioned previously, language is extremely important to our formation of concepts and especially our understanding of the world around us. Language is the tool that connects the individual to the group through socialization. We discussed in Chapter 5, "Relationship Skills," how this works from caregiver to infant and from adults interacting with each other to create shared meaning and synchronous concepts. Social construction is based upon several assumptions:

- We understand our world based upon how we interpret our experiences.
- How we interpret current experiences is based upon past experiences.
- Language, culture, and family impact our past experiences.
- How we interact with the world is colored by language, culture, and family.

These assumptions bring us to two conclusions. First, how we see the world (our reality) is true for us and that acting out this truth can make it so. Second, our actions are in service to support this truth. Essentially, interpretation of our experiences (which is based on past experiences, language, culture, and family) affects how we interact with the world (our actions and decisions). This is the foundation of our reality. This theory underscores the significance of language in forming our concepts and our mental model of the world. It also aids in understanding how concepts and mental models can differ from culture to culture.

So, how does this theory help us understand decision making? Our decisions are based upon how we see the world or more specifically our concept of the world, which is our truth. We act in service to this truth. The part where we can make a significant impact is how we interpret our experiences. Therefore, tools that can help us interpret more effectively will help us improve our decision making.

Developing Problem-Solving Concepts

Using strategies that help to create shared concepts to make better decisions is extremely useful. As mentioned earlier in Chapter 3, "Self-Management," strategies that provide a structure to problem solving are extremely useful, especially when used across multiple contexts. For example, a calming-down strategy combined with some problem-solving steps allows for common language to describe and facilitate the decision making process. If you do an internet search on "basic problem-solving steps," you will find numerous examples of routines, and there are common elements in all.

1. Identify and articulate the problem.
2. Brainstorm various ways to solve the problem.
3. Evaluate possible solutions.
4. Pick a course of action.
5. Try it out.
6. Evaluate the outcome.

Numerous programs utilize these shared concept strategies and regardless of the number of steps they use, they are proven to be highly effective in aiding students in improved problem-solving skills.

Our body budget impacts our decision making, so make sure to add a question about your physical state, such as:

Are physical needs affecting a prediction of emotion?

For example, you might experience an instant of frustration or strong irritability and think *"Well, it's because of what my friend just said to me."* But. . .maybe you're just hungry and it's well past lunchtime. Or maybe you are feeling down today and you don't know why. How have you been sleeping? Have you been eating well? Have you been getting enough exercise? Have you been drinking enough water? So, when considering our emotional state, thinking about physical information, past experiences, and current situations may be helpful in the decision-making process.

Decision Making in Action: Integrating Ethics into SEL

SEE Learning™ (https://seelearning.emory.edu) is a K–12 social, emotional, and ethical learning program that was developed at Emory University's Center for Contemplative

Science and Compassion-Based Ethics in collaboration with His Holiness the Dalai Lama. In addition to the CASEL competencies, the SEE Learning program enhances SEL programming with key additional components, which includes: attention training, compassion, ethical discernment, resilience, and trauma-informed practice.

Reshma Piramal is the Co-Head of Operations for SEE Learning in India.

SEL Around the World: 10 Questions with Reshma Piramal

1. **How did you become involved in SEE Learning?**
I did my bachelor's degree in India in speech and language therapy. I moved to the UK to do my master's with a specialization in developmental speech and language therapy. The UK has a community-based model, where children are not looked at in isolation. When I came back to India, I worked with kids in rural areas and realized that I am only one person, but I can work with teachers and parents to train the caregiver to support the child in the absence of specialist intervention. I began to recognize the value of empowering others on their journey toward the development of praxis [practice]. The SEE Learning model is very similar – a train-the-trainer model that supports the journey of an educator as a facilitator in the classroom, cultivating skills in their students so that they are eventually embodied. From the very beginning when the SEE Learning curriculum was launched, it was almost a coming together of all the things I was passionate about – empowering educators to help grow skills of compassion, resiliency, and interdependence in their students while transforming themselves. While the curriculum is articulated as learning experiences, they are at their core a set of practices that need to be revisited if they are to be eventually embodied. We work with students by empowering the educators. The SEE Learning Program provides opportunities to reflect and develop critical insight/*aha* moments and then practice. It was like revisiting something I was familiar with. I see how critical it is for us to engage and empower teachers to reimagine the education landscape teaching skills that are vital in this day and age.

(*continued*)

I've been in this role since SEE Learning was globally launched in 2019.

2. **How is SEE Learning different from other SEL Programs?**
   The focus of much of contemporary education is about academic and economic success with little or no focus on human flourishing. Certain skills, such as *resilience* and *compassion*, are no longer a luxury – they are a necessity. This has been amplified by the tragic COVID situation we have all faced together. What is special and sets SEE apart is this focus on cultivating skills that innately exist in each one of us and that are at the core of so many others we define and value as SEL skills. Building on attention training and through a trauma-informed, resilience-based approach, SEE Learning ensures the optimization of learning any new skill. Establishing awareness and focus and security priming through a resiliency-informed approach is an essential first step. Learning cannot happen without this. Building on this readiness, SEE Learning introduces the lens of compassion as the guiding principle of all that we do. Motivation is key. Eventually the purpose is that all that we engage in is informed by a deep embodied understanding of the interdependence nature of things – *a systems-thinking approach.*
   Attention training, resilience, compassion, and systems thinking are the key differentiators that are introduced as a set of practices to help educators gain familiarity and proficiency while providing opportunities to reflect and gain critical insight so that these skills are eventually embedded into practice.
3. **How inclusive or accessible is SEE?**
   His Holiness the Dalai Lama has been very interested in the dialogue between science and ancient-wisdom contemplative traditions. In his 2011 book, *Beyond Religion, Ethics for a Whole World,* he talks about an ethics-based approach focused on universal human values instead of religious ones. We live in a volatile world. Pandemics. Wars. Climate change. Humanity has always been confronted with challenges, they were there before, and they will continue to be there moving ahead. We must learn how best to navigate through these tumultuous times with wisdom and compassion so that the choices we make are beneficial to

(*continued*)

all as a community. How do we cultivate compassion, resilience, tolerance and understand our shared common humanity? How do you equip students with these skills and articulate this broad vision into a classroom pedagogy that is agnostic of differences and founded in basic human values of flourishing? It is with this motivation and secular essence that the SEE Learning Program was conceptualized and designed while keeping in mind grade level appropriateness. It's also an open-source program – anyone can access it free of charge.

4. **What role does ethics play in SEL?**
   No one really talks about ethics as an integral part of SEL, but it is a critical component of why we do what we do, the choices we make and our motivation behind it. His Holiness the Dalai Lama says that kindness won't save the world, but kindness with wisdom is what makes all the difference. Guided by compassion not just for ourselves but for others helps create a culture of inclusion, affection, gratitude, and empathy. This foundational understanding while being aware of the motivation behind the choices we make, moves us from a focus on the self, to other focus and eventually to a community focus. A systems-thinking approach that recognizes interdependence where we move from thinking of ourselves as an island to being part of a larger community where everyone benefits. This is the key to human flourishing. SEL without the "why" is just like bandaging a bleeding wound without addressing the festering infection.
5. **How important is educator training in SEE Learning?**
   Educator training and capacity building is a key part of the SEE Learning Program. You can't teach someone a skill that you haven't mastered yourself. Just like you would learn to play the guitar before you teach your students how to play one, teachers need to explore, understand, and reflect on practices they wish to see embodied in their students. Although the SEE Learning curriculum makes learning experiences accessible, teachers need to explore the content themselves, not just read the script and transact it. We help by providing teachers with opportunities to build for direct experiences and opportunities to grow themselves. We focus on supporting educators as they facilitate

(*continued*)

and implement the program in their classrooms. Our endeavor isn't just supporting the "how" to deliver, but also opportunities to develop critical insights, so that practices are eventually embodied in the classroom. Teachers must walk the talk. Empowered teachers are able to take learning experiences both authentically and with fidelity to the program. We recognize teachers as emotional contagions. Research tells us that in equations of power dynamics the one that wields greater power is more likely to influence the other. So, educators who model embodied compassion have a direct impact on the wellbeing of their classrooms. Children pick up on these things. It's like a seed that lies under the soil. There has to be adequate sunlight, water nutrients in the soil, etc., to enable the seed to grow into a robust tree. The idea is to create an ecosystem so that the values and skills we hope to see grow become second nature to who you are. The approach is to say "Hey, you have resilience, you have these strengths, how can we help you access what's innate in you?" We want educators to be "guides on the side" rather than a "sage on the stage."

6. **What feedback about the program have you received from teachers?**
   We launched globally in 2019. Over 2,000 teachers have been oriented and trained. Hundreds of people are deeply immersed in this learning. There has been an overwhelming response of positive feedback. Testimonials from teachers on how transformational SEE Learning has been in their lives and how their classroom culture has shifted with students exhibiting awareness and self-regulation have been shared. Some schools have reported students asking for more SEE Learning time. Students have also brought their learning home from parent reports. Similarly, teachers talked about how the skills they have learned have been used in their everyday dealings outside the classroom. We're waiting on research studies just embarked on in Columbia, Brazil, and India to deeply understand fidelity of implementation and look for emerging indicators that might begin to show impacts.

7. **How do students view SEL? Parents?**
   In one example a teacher provided, a student who won a sporting contest reported that self-regulation

(*continued*)

strategies clearly helped them stay resilient through the competition. There is so much uncertainty. So much anxiety. PTSD. A lot of kids appreciate being able to know they have the option to bring them back to a zone of wellbeing when they are bumped off by triggers and events in everyday life.

SEE Learning has not created content for parents just yet. It does have guidelines for disseminating information to parents. Practices during COVID times (resilience, compassion) have been shared with students and parents. Some schools and organizations have told us that parents have expressed appreciation for the resources that introduce resilience skills.

8. **Has the pandemic changed the view of SEL?**
SEL is now a buzzword. The pandemic has made its urgency felt perhaps. Suddenly, for the first time, there's a direct experience. Teachers have seen the disruption that the pandemic has caused on our wellbeing both mental and physical. Schools have reached out. Not everyone may use the word *SEL*, but they know it's an important need. From the perspective of the Indian state governments, they are grappling with how to deal with closed schools [during the pandemic] for over a year and a half for most students. Digital access is limited in India. There is a deep need for SEL to go beyond just delivery at scale. Many stakeholders are focused on delivery of certain SEL skills to students without the work on oneself. If SEL skills are to be sustainable, they must be integrated as classroom practices that go beyond a rescue remedy. There needs to be a shift in understanding SEL as skills to be cultivated before they can be generalized.

9. **What SEL domain or skill do you think is the MOST important for students to master in order to be successful in life?**
Self-awareness. It begins and ends there. Most of us navigate through life and interact with others with little sense of our impact on the outside world. By building self-awareness first, we can then begin to regulate our emotions. We can then think about others and move gradually outward with another focus. With this awareness, we learn about our impact on the collective and how to engage with the external world meaningfully so that there is benefit to all. SELF-AWARENESS holds it all together. You cannot expect to support

(*continued*)

others if you can't help yourself. Self-awareness is the first step and most important. This then helps us set our motivation as well, which is crucial.

10. **What's something you wish everyone knew about SEL?**
We have to stop treating SEL as a separate offering and treat it as the DNA or fabric of our engagement in schools. A colleague recently very beautifully articulated how in India we have a plate with different bowls of food. We don't eat just one dish; we eat several things. We need to think of SEL as the entire plate. In essence it's how we engage with the world – not just in the classroom, but outside the classroom. I wish people would understand this and not treat it in isolation. It is core to how we engage with and interact with our students.

Improve Your Classroom Practice

If you think your decision making could use a little improvement, try one of these three strategies!

- **Utilize a Decision-Making Process**
  Remember, there are plenty of decision-making routines to choose from! Pick one and implement it. Model making choices in front of your students and think aloud when making a collective group decision. You might wish to consider using the strategy on the following page, but whatever you select, your routine should:
  - Help articulate the precise decision to be made.
  - Evaluate the options, including pros and cons.
  - Consider what's going on physically – why does my brain predict that information?
    - What impact does the way I'm feeling have on making decisions?
    - Does this feel like something from your past?
    - A problem with a friend might feel different from a past situation based on environmental inputs.
    - Is it justified or is it a prediction error? Just because you feel this way does not mean that it is right.
  - Implement the decision and then assess and evaluate your choice.

Decision-Making Process

Step 1. What is the decision you have to make?

____

____

____

Step 2. What information do you need to make the decision?

____

____

____

Step 3. What are your options?

____

____

____

Step 4. What are the consequences of each choice?

____

____

____

Step 5. How do you feel emotionally and physically? How does this information affect your perception of the decision-making process?

____

____

____

Step 6. Make a decision and try it out.

____

____

____

Step 7. Assess and evaluate your choice.
Did it work? GREAT!
If not, go back to Step 3.

- **Identify Core Values**

  An important part of decision making is being able to identify your core values. When you know what's most important to you, you can make sure your decisions align with those core values. It can be challenging to teach students about values and help them identify what their values are without it being interpreted as teaching students what their values should be.

  One way to successfully accomplish this goal is by doing character analysis using texts. You can ask students to identify traits of a character and then explain, "*Some of these characteristics you've described (honesty, fairness) are called values. When we talk about values, we are not talking about material things like phones or designer clothing or video games. Values are the ideas or beliefs that are most important to us in life.*" If possible, link the character's values to a decision. For example, in the book *The Boy Who Harnessed the Wind* by William Kamkwamba, wisdom was an important core value, so the main character decided to continue his own education even though his family could not afford to pay for his formal schooling.

  Further, you can use the graphic organizer in the following table to help students identify their values. Make sure to explain that everyone has values, but not everyone has the same values. Values might be different based on where you live, your family, your religion, or your age. Some examples of values are honesty, fairness, and respect. Knowing what our values are is important because it helps us do the right thing. It can be a little overwhelming to think of our values. How do we decide what is most important to us in life? How do we know the beliefs and ideas that guide how we live, the people we want to be, and the friends we make? This work is crucial because understanding what our values are helps us make decisions that honor what is important to us. You may even want to complete the Core Values worksheet yourself!

Core Values

Use the list that follows to determine the 5 core values that are most important to you. Rate each core value on a scale of 0–3:

0 = not important at all
1 = somewhat important
2 = important to you
3 = very important

Once you've rated all of the core values, find the ones that have the highest rating and prioritize those to make a list of 5 core values. Your list of 5 should be prioritized with 1 being the most important to you and 5 being the least important to you.

Courage/ Bravery ___	Citizenship ___	Generous ___
Persistence/ Perseverance ___	Gratitude ___	Emotional intelligence ___
Honesty/ Integrity ___	Optimism ___	Forgiveness ___
Enthusiasm ___	Sense of humor ___	Modesty and humility ___
Teamwork ___	Appreciating the arts ___	Exercising self-control ___
Leadership ___	Having a purpose ___	Cautious ___
Social responsibility ___	Giving and receiving love ___	Creative ___
Fairness ___	Kindness and compassion ___	Curious ___
Open-minded ___	Wise ___	Having perspective ___
Other: ___	Other: ___	Other: ___

(*continued*)

Core Values (*continued*)

Fill in your top 5 core values listed in order of importance below. Hint: You may need to eliminate some if you had more than 5 with the highest rating.

1.

2.

3.

4.

5.

- **Choices and Consequences**
  It may sound obvious, but we are all models for our children and students. One of the best ways to help students develop decision-making skills is by giving them appropriate choices and consequences that matter. Let's look at each in more detail.

Giving Appropriate Choices

The important thing to remember when we are giving students appropriate choices is that the options must be equal in value. If they are not equal, then what we are doing is trying to manipulate the child. We hope that by providing reasonable options, they will make a good choice. An example of this might be "You can sit on the carpet, or you can bring your chair to the carpet to sit on." A manipulative choice might be "You can sit on the carpet, or you can go sit in the office." Clearly these choices are not equal as one of the choices most likely will be seen as a punishment. We want to avoid these types of choices for students so they will learn to make the best decisions.

Consequences that Matter

The important thing to remember about this strategy is that the consequence has to matter to the student, or it will not be an effective teachable moment. Here's an example: "If you don't hurry and get your coat on, you might miss the bus." If a child doesn't like taking the bus, or perhaps really loves being in your class or a number of other explanations, you can see that "missing the bus" might just be what they had in mind. You have to know what motivates your students in order for the strategy to be effective.

By modeling appropriate choices and consequences that matter, the hope is that students will use these strategies in their own decision-making process.

Reflect on Decision Making

Please take a moment to spend some time thinking deeply on each of the questions below. Remember, these responses are just for you, so be honest in your responses.

Reflect on a decision you made recently. How do you feel about it?

How did you feel emotionally and physically? How did it affect the decision-making process?

What process do you use when it comes to making decisions?

What would you like to improve in the area of responsible decision making?

How will you go about improving the area you identified? What immediate steps or actions will you take?

___

___

___

___

___

SEL for All Students

When we say "SEL for ALL Students," what does that mean to you? For us, it doesn't look much different than what a traditional classroom looks like, with teachers doing their best to differentiate instruction for every student. But some people get hung up on the SEL part of the learning experience, so let's look at how we can ensure SEL is taught in an equitable manner to students with disabilities, those who are learning English, and our gifted students.

Students with Autism

The implications of the new research for students with disabilities is ongoing but impactful, particularly for students with Autism Spectrum Disorder (ASD). The Theory of Constructed Emotion challenges the current interventions based on classical theories of emotions. Dr. Lisa Feldman Barrett's work shows that contrary to what we have been teaching students, there are no universal expressions of, nor physiological responses to, emotion. This may come as a huge relief to parents and teachers who felt pressured to teach students with disabilities specific ways to show and recognize emotions.

Dr. Barrett is uniquely sympathetic toward parents of autistic children. She is frustrated by the fact that the "classical views of emotion are guiding policies and practices that actively harm people." Specifically, those interventions which hold that if children can recognize basic emotional expressions on the faces of others, they will be better able to function in the world. While children with ASD are able to learn to identify specific expressions in laboratory situations, it does not always translate outside of these settings. However, current interventions utilized in classrooms, such as teaching specific facial cues to correspond with feelings labels, are still widely used. Practices like these can make students and teachers feel like failures and give false hope to parents, caregivers, and those children with ASD.

New research is emerging on ASD and construction, specifically in the area of prediction. Dr. Pawan Sinha and his colleagues hypothesize that ASD is a disorder of prediction. To explain, they give an example of the experience of a magic show. The brain uses information from the body, the current situation, and its concepts and makes predictions. Because our brains are so good at predicting, magicians have to work exceptionally hard to trick us. We are surprised and amazed by magic because the magician makes something that seems impossible, possible; what we expect to happen does not – our predictions are wrong. This type of experience is pleasing because of the occasional nature of attending a magic show.

What would it be like if every day felt like a magic show? Daily occurrences might seem magical, constantly surprising, and without cause. They compare the experience of autism to a "magical phenomenon." If that were the case, an unpredictable world might feel overwhelming.

There are several "significant correlates of autism" that might be explained by the theory of Predictive Impairment in Autism (PIA) – insistence on sameness, sensory hypersensitivity, interacting with the dynamic world, theory of the mind challenges, and enhanced proficiencies.

Nearly one-third of those with ASD possess the trait of "insistence of sameness," and one aspect of sameness is a reliance upon rituals. Unpredictability can increase anxiety. Research shows that there is a correlation between increased anxiety and ritualistic behavior. These types of behaviors, such as washing hands, turning the light switch on and off several times before leaving a room, or self-stimulating behaviors (known as stimming) serve to provide a calming response. Imposing rigid structure of sameness and stimming helps to decrease the anxiety of unpredictability.

Almost 90% of all ASD children report challenges with sensory stimulus or hypersensitivity. For many of us, the more we experience something, the more we become habituated to that experience – it loses its novelty because we begin to predict its occurrence. However, if we have problems predicting, the thing that was irritating at first remains irritating because it remains novel. An example might be a tag on the back of your shirt. It might have been bothersome to you the first time you wore it, but over time, you forget that it's there. For someone with ASD, they never get used to the tag. It is irksome to them every time they wear the shirt.

Many people with ASD (nearly 75%) never learn to drive. Driving is an example of a dynamic experience, where movement is an integral aspect. Again, we can see that if there are prediction problems, driving would be a difficult task. Prediction skills are needed to anticipate what others will do while driving and where your car is likely to be in relation to other cars in motion.

Theory of mind is a concept that helps explain how we understand other people, which is a crucial skill when interacting with others. It requires us to be able to think about the other person, consider what we know about them and use that knowledge to predict why they might be acting in a certain way, or how they might act in certain situations in the future. Prediction is a necessary aspect of theory of mind, and if you have difficulty predicting what someone might do, or why they might act a certain way, social interactions might be challenging.

So, what can we do to provide support to students with ASD? There are three main approaches to intervention: Applied Behavioral Analysis (ABA), Developmental Relationship-Based Intervention (DRBI), and Naturalistic Developmental Behavioral Intervention (NDBI). It is not our intention to discuss the merits or contrast and compare the methodologies and the associated research.

When selecting a program, consider:

- The child and family,
- The issues that they want to be addressed with treatment,
- Accessibility – and to keep in mind that there is no magic bullet solution to address such a complex issue.

Autism *is* a complex issue, which requires a variety of interventions. However, there are some basic suggestions for what we can all do to affect the predictions that our brains make:

1. Take care of your body budget by getting good sleep, nutrition, and exercise.
2. Work on developing your concepts – emotional granularity.
3. Develop new concepts.
4. Talk about body sensations and emotional sensations – the cause and what to do about them.

English Language Learners

As we've mentioned in earlier chapters, teaching SEL is similar to teaching language acquisition. Teaching students who are learning English social emotional skills isn't much different than any other subject. Here are some research-based best practices you can use:

1. **Teach vocabulary explicitly:** You'll need to explicitly teach emotion vocabulary and remember that there may be emotion words in other languages that don't exist or translate into English.
2. **Frequent formative assessment:** Check in with students to make sure that they understand what they've learned with frequent informal assessments. Reteach if needed. You can accomplish this easily with Exit Slips.
3. **Build relationships:** One of the cornerstones of the CASEL framework is the relationships skills domain. Model it by building strong, positive relationships with your students. You can also extend that to building relationships with your students' families and the greater community. Ask questions about their culture, language, holidays, and celebrations.
4. **Use a strengths-based approach:** Remember that English learners have many strengths. Look for what they bring to the classroom, including cultural and linguistic assets. Encourage students to share their ideas and provide opportunities to let them show off what they know.
5. **Create a welcoming classroom environment:** Work with students to create a welcoming physical space in which they can use their voice to express their identity. By expressing an interest in your students' culture, it shows you value them.

Extra Enrichment

When it comes to meeting all the demands of the classroom, it's often easy to overlook the "gifted" students. These are usually the amenable students who grasp the content most easily, complete the assignments accurately and expeditiously, and are eager to build their knowledge.

Providing enrichment opportunities and activities for these students can be challenging in any classroom – even one where you're teaching SEL. However, there are some effective ways to engage those students in your SEL class.

The first step is to understand the gifted student's talents and interests. Once you have that knowledge, it's easier to tailor activities that will engage and motivate them.

For example:

- Artistic students could write or draw something related to the SEL concept being taught. Or they could write a script about a conflict and produce it in the classroom.
- Encourage students to move beyond the skill they're learning and apply it in the real world. For example, they can explore how empathy can affect a doctor or architect, or how scientists use problem-solving strategies to find cures for diseases.
- Challenge students to have them extend and enrich their learning by utilizing other resources (library, internet, etc.) to research a topic and share their findings with the class.
- Partner your gifted students with older student mentors who can help them focus on developing specific skills and interests.

Implementing SEL in First Nation Communities: An Interview with Terri-Anne Larry of the Mi'kmaq Nation

Terri-Anne Larry is a Mi'kmaq Principal of Natoaganeg School, a preschool, K–8 school in Eel Ground, New Brunswick, Canada. In 2017, she was the program champion for a two-year pilot study by the First Nation Education Initiative, Inc. (FNEII) to evaluate the implementation of the PATHS® social emotional learning (SEL) program in elementary schools in First Nation communities in New Brunswick, Canada. We checked in with her five years later to see how things are going and learn about SEL and First Nations culture.

1. **What successes have you seen as a result of the implementation of SEL programming in your district?** We have so many examples over the past five years on how much SEL programming has helped our kids and staff to manage big feelings, problem solve, and to develop healthier relationships and ways of coping.

   For example, we have been experiencing a lot of conflict in some classes with both boys and girls. Of course, they have unique challenges. We had to set some ground rules because we kept dealing with the same issues daily, and it didn't seem there was going to be any resolving. As a team, we told them that not everyone needs to get along, but you have to respect each other. We used terminology to introduce the concept that you can repair friendships, forgive, etc. This program gives them alternative options. It opens the door to solve and mend conflicts. We didn't dismiss the way students felt, but we continued to provide a space for activities where everyone is included. As we were getting ready for an event, one student actually made a bracelet for another student without being prompted to do so. I feel that is progress.

   One boy who has typically been physically aggressive during conflict has learned how to express himself instead of using force. We've seen progress on managing his feelings and also experiencing remorse and regret.

   When I first became principal, I had kids in my office all the time and we were experiencing so many changes at once that it seemed that it was hard for everyone to cope. Now, I feel that the teachers are more able to handle conflicts and work through some problems. Some teachers are really relying on PATHS® daily. They have incorporated PATHS® throughout their whole day and have invested a lot of time to implement the program. There were some students who made some bad choices, and their peers were worried about them and shared it with their teacher. The teacher came to me and I brought the students in. These students didn't typically get into trouble. They actually were part of our first group to have PATHS® since Kindergarten. I didn't even have to go as far as questioning the students because they talked out everything in front of me. They shared how they were disappointed in themselves, and how they learned their lesson and shared more of what they were going through. After our discussion, they knew there would still be a consequence and they accepted it. And I did not see these students again in my office. SEL has really helped a lot of kids on so many levels.

2. **What do your students think about SEL?**
   Some kids are harder to reach as far as wanting to share their feelings, but we have seen a lot of behaviors turn around. There are some kids that still refuse to talk about stuff that is bothering them and that is okay. We had one student in particular who did shut down a lot. This student didn't like a lot of attention or drama. However, they were extremely artistic. A teacher picked up on it and shared it with other staff members. Pretty soon more people were acknowledging the artistic talents and then that turned into more compliance. She became our turnaround student that year. This year, we have two turnaround students, who were both described as developing more social emotional skills, communicating better with adults, and are making new friends. I feel that it is amazing that the SEL skills were acknowledged as a strength and are good skills to have.
3. **How is SEL responsive to First Nations culture?**
   Cultural teaching and SEL fit well together. I feel that for me it was a very good way to bridge the gap between my cultural and spiritual world. For example: Focusing on self-awareness – being true to yourself, looking at the differences and uniqueness that everyone has. Not everyone who works here is from our community, but we all bring something to the table. SEL is our common ground. Common lingo. We can take the concepts, and everyone can bring themselves into the lessons. I feel that in our culture we are so connected to animals and the fact that Twiggle [the turtle] and the characters are animals is really great. In our community we have some other animals that are close to our culture, and we can include our seven sacred teachings and use animals such as the eagle, bear, moose, fox, etc.
4. **What are some of the ways you implement SEL into the school day?**
   We have sort of taken the teachings of SEL and have used it as a tiered system in our school. We have our classroom teachers who implement the curriculum, and we also have a guidance counselor who works with the kids to develop the SEL skills in a more intensive environment. She works with groups of kids or the whole class to further touch on some topics. During morning announcements, we have a PATHS® thought of the day and we announce a PATHS® Staff of the day. We want to continue to encourage giving and receiving compliments and acknowledging our own strengths. We recently celebrated our first Pride Day – to show that we are all special and unique. This really is just a great way to end the year with our classroom parties in the classrooms.

5. **What's the *Staff of the Day* routine?**
In the hallway, we have a bulletin board, where we posted a picture of a staff member and everyone wrote compliments about them. At the beginning and end of the day, we'd make an announcement on the PA about the compliments. Many staff members have shared that they really didn't feel they needed to be a part of it but when they heard the announcements it did make them feel good.
6. **What are some of the unique issues facing your students?**
As a First Nations school we have many challenges that affect our kids on so many levels. We are probably described as being from a low socioeconomic population, high suicide rates, high diabetes rates, etc. We have a legacy of residential schools that we must deal with, overcome, and make sure the same mistakes never happen. This year for Orange Shirt Day (an event every September 30 that recognizes the First Nations survivors of residential schools in Canada), we had a survivor's daughter share how she remembered her mother talking about the lack of food and experiments conducted. Sometimes our events can bring up a lot of emotions not only for our students but for our staff, guests, and community members too. What we know about the residential school children is they didn't have a voice, they didn't feel wanted, they were neglected. They didn't feel human. Trying to take that experience, we wanted to show that all children matter, we all matter. With the recent recoveries of the bodies of students, some of our kids felt sick to their stomachs about it. They shared it. One student felt so sick, he had to go home. This student also shared this to their parent. I felt it was healing.
A couple of students are identifying as gender neutral – it's new for kids to come to us with this. The teachers are open to using different pronouns and names. This is the healthiest option for the student. It's the best way to engage the student. When students don't feel that they can come to school, we really need to get to the bottom of it or try. Sometimes the problems are quite complex, and we need outside resources to help but sometimes the students just want to feel heard. We need to try and encourage that some students have different styles and tastes. It's all okay. Covid has been rough on everyone, but I feel that when we celebrated our Pride Day, everyone was happy and excited. It was so nice to see kids so happy!
7. **How do you engage with students' families?**
Parents are receptive and we are still trying to educate and build awareness about SEL. I feel it has helped me to talk to parents about difficult topics by using some of the

terminology. It has helped me to not be afraid to reach out and validate their feelings – it's coming more naturally. Not just for me – for everybody.

8. **What challenges have you faced when it comes to implementing SEL into your school?**
   When we first presented the concept of SEL at the time it was a little hard. The teachers did not have any experience in SEL and I think some felt that we are educators not social workers. But everyone has feelings and for me realizing that we all need good communication skills, interpersonal skills to accomplish our goals in a team setting is so important. And we all need a way to learn, develop, and practice these skills. Bringing in the SEL curriculum has helped. Personally, I feel it has changed my whole outlook on education. It needs to be a pillar in education.
9. **When identifying potential teachers to work at your school, is SEL one of your considerations?**
   In our interviews, we do ask about SEL and their knowledge. We promote SEL as a selling point for some new teachers. It's okay if they are not familiar, but we hope they see the benefit and share that they will be guided. A teacher who thinks SEL is a burden or doesn't see the value wouldn't be chosen.
10. **In what ways do you continue to work on your SEL skills and develop your staff's SEL skills?**
    I still feel that more work needs to be done in SEL, not only in our school but in the community. I am working on myself and trying to find ways to mesh my cultural teachings and SEL. As an administrator, our team gave teachers summer readings in social emotional learning, mindfulness, and meditation. We have a good team, and they believe in SEL.

CHAPTER 8

SEL in Every Content Area

While it's easy to buy into why SEL should be taught in the classroom, the idea of implementing SEL may seem daunting. In this chapter, we'll show you how to easily incorporate social emotional learning into the lesson plan of any subject. In fact, chances are that you are already doing some social emotional learning in your classroom.

Self-Awareness

1. **You welcome students at the door of your classroom.** You may not realize it but greeting your students at the door every day and asking them how they're doing not only builds relationships (more on this later), but it also forces them to build self-awareness. By simply asking how they're doing or noticing when something doesn't seem right, students can identify and reflect on what they are feeling and why. This builds emotion vocabulary and self-awareness.
2. **You do a bell ringer/warm-up/do-now activity to start your class.** Many of the teachers we spoke with start their classes with an activity to get their students in the zone. Whatever you call it, if you occasionally take the opportunity to ask questions to build self-awareness, then you're doing SEL! For example, you can start by asking students to list three positive things that happened to them, three positive traits, or write about something that's bothering them. You can also start the class with a mindfulness activity, such as the mindful minute, or by creating a zentangle or a mandala. These are easy SEL activities that you can do in any core academic classroom.
3. **Your students write in a journal.** You may think that writing in a journal is only for English class. But you'd be surprised to learn that journaling has been found to have benefits in every academic subject area. Journaling builds trust, helps some students to

organize their thoughts better, allows for self-reflection, questioning, and exploration. And it's also a way for you to learn more about your students. Some tips for journaling are to be consistent as to how often you do it and to provide prompts.

One teacher described a weekly journal entry routine called "Glow and Grow." During this exercise, students had to identify one thing they did well during the week, and one thing they still needed to develop. It could be school related or personal. This kind of self-reflection was really helpful for the teacher because they could identify things the student needed help with and also a great self-awareness activity for students.

4. **You give genuine compliments like it's your job.** There's a ton of research about the power of compliments. Not only does giving compliments benefit the recipient, but also the person giving the compliments. You can do specific routines where you give students compliments on a set schedule or find opportunities to catch them and give a genuine compliment.

One teacher described the following experience: "I noticed, quite early on, that students had no problem listing all the things they were "bad" at. But finding things they were good at was much harder. I thought hard about how to get students to think about things they were good at, but they still had a difficult time finding nice things to say about themselves. Finally, I had an *aha!* moment in the classroom while we were discussing the idea of giving and receiving compliments. One student was struggling with something nice to say about himself. Another student chimed in, "Marcos helped me when my car wouldn't start. He's really good with cars." Then, Marcos responded to the compliment with a compliment of his own: "Well, you helped me with math. You're really smart at math." Then another student added, "Genesis is good at math, too! And biology! She's going to be a doctor." Before I knew it, this whole crazy compliment circle was happening. Every student left class that day feeling good about themselves. I just stood back in awe as the students taught this SEL "lesson." We ended up creating a compliment jar activity once a week. We'd draw a name, and everyone (including the teacher) wrote one compliment for the person on a sticky note. Once all the anonymous compliments were received, I'd read them aloud and then give the stack of compliments to the students to keep. That way the next time they needed an idea for something they were good at, they had an entire list of about 30 to pick from."

Self-Management

Do you use any strategies in your classroom to help students self-regulate? Maybe they need help settling down after an exciting assembly or you want them to get excited about an upcoming project? Or maybe you allow them to take a personal time out if they're feeling frustrated, anxious, or otherwise unable to cooperate or participate in your classroom? Guess what? These are all examples of SEL.

In addition to working with students to teach self-regulation strategies at the beginning of the year, another way to integrate SEL is by setting personal academic goals. At the beginning of the year, after looking at their placement, assessment, and Individualized Education Program (if applicable), consider holding individual conferences with each student. During the conference, collaboratively work to set three achievable academic goals for the year. Those goals might be to submit a science fair project, read 10 books, or take the AP Calculus exam.

Make sure to follow up with your students quarterly to see where they are, set new goals, celebrate any goals they've already met, or strategize different ways to meet the goals that haven't been obtained yet. You can also utilize the SMART Goals lesson and resources as outlined in Chapter 9, "SEL Lesson Plans and Novel Study Ideas."

You can save time by doing the quarterly check-ins as a journal prompt or as a Do-Now/Wrap-Up activity. Doing this will result in positive benefits. Not only is goal setting and individual conferencing with students helpful in getting students invested and motivated in their own learning, but it also helps build relationships and expands their social emotional learning skills in the self-management domain.

You can use the graphic organizer in the Resources section of the book to track these meetings.

Social Awareness

Having social awareness isn't always easy for students! But there are some ways to integrate social awareness into your classroom. One of the easiest ways is to integrate diverse texts across all subjects. Look for mathematicians or scientists from underrepresented groups (check out https://www.NobelPrize.org for suggestions). Look at historical events and consider them from a different perspective. The website and magazine found at https://www.learningforJustice.org has great ideas for how to do this.

For example, one teacher recounted how her students, who were English learners from Hispanic countries living in the northeast, read Julia Alvarez's book *In the Time of the Butterflies,* which is historical fiction based on life in the Dominican Republic. This assignment forced students to think about what life might have been like for their relatives under the Trujillo administration. It also gave them a topic to engage with their parents and other relatives. For an assignment, some students wrote very moving interviews they conducted with relatives about those times. One family member explained to me that although she initially never wanted to think about it, she was glad to share the stories with her nephew so he could understand "why they left." That's something you just can't teach in a classroom.

Diversity encompasses race, ethnicity, gender, sexual orientation, socioeconomic status, age, physical abilities, and religious or political beliefs. The concept of diversity encourages acceptance and respect to build empathy and compassion. Having a diverse classroom means recognizing that everyone is unique and respecting and appreciating those individual differences.

Keep in mind that social awareness isn't just about diversity. It's understanding the social context in which you find yourself and having the skills necessary to navigate that context effectively. It's being able to recognize what's expected of you in given situations and acting accordingly. The ability to do this requires an understanding of the culture and community as well as the individual(s) and this is not just for differing cultures but for our own culture as well. What are the norms of various situations? Do we act the same with our friends as we do with our work colleagues or with older community members? Understanding what the expectations are in given situations is key to navigating these situations successfully. Spending time talking about how to manage various situations and roleplaying options can be effective in helping students prepare for new experiences.

Finally, exploring these differences should take place in a safe and positive environment, where respectful questioning is encouraged. This may take setting some guidelines and putting them in place in advance for students to practice. This might include discussion protocols to make sure everyone feels heard and respected – even if they didn't agree on a subject. Facing History and Ourselves has some helpful resources, which can be found at: https://www.facinghistory.org/resource-library/facing-ferguson-news-literacy-digital-age/preparing-students-difficult/.

Relationship Skills

Do you do group activities and projects in your classroom? If so, you'll be happy to know that having students work in groups or teams is one way to discreetly build relationship skills. When students work in teams, they build important skills, such as:

- Developing healthy relationships
- Teamwork and collaboration
- Problem-solving and conflict resolution
- Leadership
- Effective communication

Another way is to build relationships with your students. An easy way to do this is with a quick emotion check-in as they enter the classroom. This doesn't require any materials or even much preparation. Simply stand at the door as your students enter and ask them how they're doing. Sure, you might want those few minutes before class starts or in between classes to prepare or grab some water, or to use the restroom. However, if you continue with this practice, you'll come to value and appreciate that time – and so will your students. In fact, as you get to know each other better, you'll know when something is wrong or when they are having a great day even without asking. These five minutes at the beginning of each class will provide insights into each of your students and will help to give you a sense of how their day is going, which will positively impact their learning in your classroom.

And don't be afraid to be vulnerable. Tell your students how you're feeling, too! This will help them to see you as an authentic human, which will build connection and trust. This doesn't mean that your students will always want to share with you what's going on. Sometimes they may not want to talk about what is bothering them at that moment but letting them know you're there for them may make them more likely to come to you later. This is SEL in action.

Building relationships with your students' families and the local community will also enrich your experience. Some ways to do this is to communicate with families about what's going on in the classroom. You can also try making calls to their homes at random intervals to report good behavior instead of waiting for something negative to happen. These positive check-ins go a long way to building connections between home and school. And, if you have to make a call to discuss a problem, you have built a positive foundation that will help families feel that you want to help rather than punish. Another way is to speak with families to identify ways they might wish to contribute to the classroom, such as speaking about a special skill, knowledge sharing, or instructing on special celebrations. Finally, use the relationships you build to help identify needs and then match them with local community resources and support for students and their families.

Responsible Decision Making

Most teachers reported that decision making was one of the more challenging SEL competencies to integrate into the classroom. Researchers estimate that children make around 3,500 decisions a day. If you have 30 students, that's tens of thousands of decisions flying around a classroom – not to mention the teacher's decisions (adults make around 35,000 decisions a day)!

It's pretty easy to implement this competency in your classroom. You can select and consistently utilize a decision-making routine, and also model decision making (think aloud when you have to make decisions). You may also want to consider using a decision matrix, such as the one here: https://asq.org/quality-resources/decision-matrix. (We're looking at you, math, and science teachers.)

Ten Questions with a Teacher: Integrating SEL Without a Curriculum

Name: Michelle T.

Subject/Grades Taught: Currently teaching high school English in Arizona, predominately to students who are English learners and those with Individualized Education Programs (IEPs).

Years Taught: Over 13 years at the middle and high school level, four years of PK intervention and enrichment.

1. **Do you think it's important to teach social emotional learning? Why or why not?**
   Yes! Social emotional learning skills are life skills, and I believe those life skills are the most important skills students need to be successful.
2. **Was SEL part of your pre-service training?**
   No, SEL was not a focus when I was getting my teaching credentials.
3. **Have you ever had any formal training in SEL?**
   In the previous district I worked in, they tried to implement an SEL program. We did a book study. Although the intent was good, the implementation did not support the teachers, so there were struggles. It initially backfired. There was no implementation plan, no teacher training, no teacher buy-in.
4. **Has your district made SEL a priority?**
   We do not have an official SEL curriculum, program, or expectations. This past year, they started addressing the need for SEL. We had some professional development to lay the groundwork to build connections/relationships with the students, but there was no consistency, no implementation plan. Administration did not make an effort to make connections to teachers. As teachers we always say we're too busy, we don't have time for it, but we made the effort with our students, but administration didn't do it with us. If you want SEL to truly extend and be part of the culture of the school, we all have to do it with each other.

(*continued*)

5. **Do you have the resources (materials, training, etc.) you need to teach SEL effectively?**
   No, I do not. I think this is a new wave in education. People are trying to catch the train (because of the pandemic) but they aren't on the track yet.

6. **How do you integrate SEL without the resources you need?**
   I use classroom texts. Being able to read texts and apply them to students' life experiences – to me, the English curriculum is the medium to teach life skills and critical thinking skills. I choose texts to help students identify with the character. I make it relevant to them, which makes it engaging so that they learn. We ask questions like:

   - How do you persevere when things are challenging?
   - How do the characters cope, adapt, work through inner conflict?

   Kids can take and learn from those examples. English is a great segue for that.

   A lot of times it's in the conversations. Predicting what a character might do, asking what the student would do in the same situation. Do you agree or disagree – why?

7. **What SEL domains (self-awareness, social awareness, decision making, relationship skills, self-management) or skills do you think are most important for students to master in order to be successful in life?**
   They all are! Self-management is difficult for students as they get older. Self-awareness and social awareness are also hard because today's students are trying to navigate peers and social media. Relationship skills are challenging because teens are trying to navigate relationships with parents as they grow. And decision making is challenging because problem solving and conflict management skills are still developing.

8. **What do your students think about SEL?**
   I think most of them are becoming more aware of mental health in general. At the middle school level, it's not always seen as a positive. A lot of emphasis is placed on depression, which is just one facet of SEL instead of the whole person. I would love for them to be able to see how they are as a person instead of just how they are surviving a situation.

(*continued*)

9. **Has parenting impacted the way you teach SEL?**
   Absolutely. Understanding the stages a child goes through is different from a formal academic setting. As parents, initially, without the SEL emphasis, you're just reacting, as opposed to trying to get through to the emotion. Without opening up a dialog, the cycle is bound to repeat itself. We hope avoiding the consequences will help them to make the right choice instead of developing the right critical thinking skills to make better choices. As a parent, you learn how to have those conversations and learn how to respond when those events are happening.
10. **What's something you wish everyone knew about SEL?**
   Understanding the five components to support the whole child, instead of just a mood or behavior. Understanding the development of SEL skills as a proactive instead of reactive approach.

CHAPTER 9

SEL Lesson Plans and Novel Study Ideas

Throughout this book, we've given ideas, stories, and tips for integrating SEL into the classroom and on improving your own knowledge base. Now it's time to take what you've learned and integrate it with these lesson plans. To show you how to do this, we've included a sample lesson for each core subject area and in each SEL competency to use as a guide. You can also download and print them at the book's web page, http://www.wiley.com/go/socialemotionalclassroom.

- Self-Awareness
- Character Strengths
- Self-Management
- SMART Goals
- Social Awareness
- Cultural Competency
- Engineering Design Challenge
- Relationships Skills
- Teamwork and Collaboration
- Decision Making
- Video Game Design Challenge

Self-Awareness Sample Lesson

This lesson plan on Character Strengths is one way to integrate self-awareness into your English language arts (ELA), health, advisory, or homeroom class times. This lesson was written for a 6th Grade classroom. You might wish to adapt the content for your students' needs based on their grade and/or development.

Character Strengths

Essential Questions: *What are strengths? How do strengths relate to self-esteem and self-confidence?*
CASEL Competency: Self-awareness, self-management
Core Subject Areas: ELA, Health
CCSS: ELA-SL.6.1, RL.6.4, L.6.5, W.6.3D
Objective: By the end of this lesson, students will be able to identify character strengths and use that knowledge to improve their overall self-confidence and self-esteem.
Approximate Time: 30 min
Key Vocabulary: Strengths, courage, justice, temperance, humanity, transcendence, perseverance
Materials:

- Character Strengths Graphic Organizer

  Warm-up: *List 3-5 things that you are good at.* Display the warm-up questions and have students write their responses on a piece of paper. Allow student volunteers to share-out some of their answers. List them on the board.

  Build background knowledge: Consider using the following videos to help build students' background knowledge about character strengths:
  - **24 Character Strengths Explained:** https://www.youtube.com/watch?v=OmlKBjkwEQU (9 min)
  - **Character Strengths 5:** https://www.youtube.com/watch?v=QzyhtPTC8bw (2 min)

Explain: *We tend to think of strength as a physical characteristic that relates to what we are able to do with our bodies. How far can a person run? How much weight can they lift? How quickly can they complete a physical task? But there are many different ways to demonstrate your strengths, or things you do well. When we know what our strengths are, it makes us feel good about ourselves and improves our confidence and self-esteem. It can also improve our self-confidence, which is the way we feel about our abilities and qualities. Let's look at the list of strengths we created during the warm-up activity.*

Ask: *What do you notice about the character strengths we identified during the warm-up?* Point out any interesting observations, such as: They are all focused on physical activities, or they are similar/different, etc.

Detail: *Distribute the Character Strengths Graphic Organizer to students.* Most character strengths can be organized into the six categories. There are many kinds of strengths, but in this lesson, we are going to focus on: Courage, Humanity, Justice, Temperance, Transcendence, and Wisdom & Knowledge. As we look at the different categories, think about the descriptors to which you can relate and provide an example for how you show that strength in the third column. Each example from the warm-up indicates a person demonstrating a different type of strength. Connect a few examples to each category, for example: [Jamal] is good at science and likes performing experiments. This falls under the wisdom & knowledge category. [Maria] demonstrates perseverance, or not giving up. This falls under the courage category. [Derek] is kind to everyone. This is part of the humanity category. [Rubin] is cautious. This is part of the temperance category. [Lucy] is a talented artist. This is part of the transcendence category. [Suleka] is a social justice warrior. This is part of the justice category. These are just some of the ways we demonstrate character strengths, but there are many others. Not everyone is going to be strong in every area, but it's important to embrace your strengths in order to build your self-esteem.

Try: *Now, work with a partner and review the criteria for each character strengths category and see if you can come up with an example for each one.* When students are done, have student volunteers share their responses.

Wrap-up: *Which character strengths are you most grateful for?* Display the wrap-up questions and have students write their responses on a piece of paper or in a reflection journal. If time permits, you can have student volunteers share their responses.

Differentiation: If necessary, pre-teach key lesson vocabulary with students using a Frye model. To extend the lesson, consider having students take the free character strengths self-assessment at: https://www.viacharacter.org/survey/account/register#youth.

To encourage the home-school connection, have students share their strengths with their family and ask them to identify other areas of strength.

Character Strengths* Graphic Organizer

Trait	Characteristics	Your Examples
Courage	• Brave • Persistent & perseverant • Honest • Enthusiastic	
Justice	• Socially responsible • Charismatic • Collaborative • Fair • Civic-minded	
Transcendence	• Grateful • Optimistic • Playful • Aesthetic • Purposeful	
Humanity	• Loving • Compassionate • Generous • Socially and emotionally intelligent	
Temperance	• Forgiving & merciful • Humble & modest • Self-controlled • Prudent & cautious	
Wisdom and Knowledge	• Creative • Curious • Open-minded • Philomathic • Perspicacious	

* Adapted from Character Strengths and Virtues, by Christopher Peterson and Martin E. P. Seligman, Oxford University Press, 2004.

Self-Management Sample Lesson

This lesson plan on SMART Goals is a great way to integrate self-management into your ELA, health, advisory, or homeroom class times. This lesson was written for a 7th Grade classroom. You may wish to adapt the content for your students' needs based on grade and development.

SMART Goals

Essential Questions: *What is a goal? What is a SMART goal? Why is it important to have SMART goals?*
CASEL Competency: Self-management, responsible decision making, self-awareness
Core subject areas: ELA, health
CCSS: ELA- SL.7.1, L.7.1, L.7.2, L.7.3, L.7.4, L.7.6, RI.7.4, W.7.4, W.7.10
Objective: By the end of this lesson students will be able to identify what a SMART goal is and why setting SMART goals is helpful. Students will also be able to identify a long-term and short-term SMART goal that they would like to set for themselves.
Approximate time: 30 min
Key Vocabulary: Goal, SMART goal, specific, measurable, attainable, relevant, timely

Materials:

- SMART Graphic Organizer

Warm-up: *Do you think it's important to have goals? Why or why not?* Display the *warm-up* questions and have students write their responses on a piece of paper. Allow student volunteers to share-out some of their answers.

Build background knowledge: Consider using the following videos to help build students' background knowledge about SMART goals:

- SMART goals – Khan Academy: https://www.youtube.com/watch?v=U4IU-y9-J8Q (3 min)
- Examples of SMART goals from students: https://www.youtube.com/watch?v=R9xMTGjsZPo&t=1s (2 min)

Explain: *Many of us are familiar with the word goal. A goal is the end result we are working toward when we set out to do something. Sometimes we set small, short-term goals for ourselves, for example, "I will turn in my homework each day this week." Other times we set bigger, more long-term goals for ourselves. For example, "I will become a musician when I grow up." Setting goals is great, as it helps us to think about what we want and what's important to us. But, if we* *want to achieve our goals, we need to make sure we have a plan. Without a plan for how to achieve our goals, we may not know where to start or what the steps look like to reach success. If* YOU *set a goal and just hope that someday it will happen, it's not very likely that you will be able to stay focused on that goal and know if you're on track to achieve it. Thankfully, there is a process that helps us to set better and more realistic goals. A SMART goal refers to an acronym that describes a process to use when we set goals. A SMART goal is a goal that is Specific, Measurable, Attainable, Relevant, and Timely. Let's talk a little about each letter and how it helps us to set better goals.*

- **Specific** means that your goal should be focused and clear. Being specific with goal setting helps you to know what exactly you're working toward so you can plan how to be successful.
- **Measurable** means that you should be able to measure your progress toward your goal and know when you've reached your goal. When goals are measurable it's easier to see if you're staying on-track.
- **Attainable** means that your goal should be realistic and something that you'll actually be able to reach. It doesn't make much sense to set a goal that you'll never be able to reach!
- **Relevant** means that your goal should be important to you and be something that you think is worth your efforts. Setting relevant goals helps you to stay motivated to achieve them.
- **Timely** means that you have an end date in your mind of when you want to achieve your goal. Having a time frame for your goal helps you to stay focused and keep your goal a priority. SMART goals are like regular goals, but with more thought put into them so that they are appropriate and help you find a clear plan for how to achieve the things you want in your life rather than just trying to "wing it."

Ask: *Sometimes it's helpful to understand a new concept by thinking about what it isn't. New Year's Eve resolutions are not typically SMART goals. How many of you make a resolution every year? How many of you achieve your resolutions? What kept you from sticking to your resolutions?* Accept student responses and discuss other non-examples of SMART goals.

Detail: *There are many areas in our lives where we can use SMART goals. We can set SMART goals for school to become better students and learners. We can set SMART goals for personal interests and extracurricular activities. We can set SMART goals for our relationships, behavior, and emotions. We can set SMART goals for improving* *our character. There's really no limit to where you can apply setting SMART goals. Today, we would like us to focus on setting one short-term SMART goal and one long-term SMART goal. A short-term SMART goal is something that you would like to achieve over the next couple of months. Some ideas for short-term SMART goals are increasing the time you spend on your homework to improve your grade in language arts, learning how to perform a specific skill for a sport or instrument that you play, having at least one positive interaction a day with family or friends, or saving up enough money to purchase an item that you want. A long-term SMART goal is something that you would like to achieve over one or two years or even longer. Some ideas for long-term SMART goals are becoming an honor roll student with consistently good grades, learning to speak a new language well enough to have a conversation, starting a business or collecting a specific amount of money for a charity, graduating middle school, high school, or college, or becoming a mentor or leader in an area that you're interested in.*

Model: *One area that I've focused a SMART goal on is becoming certified as a school administrator. (Feel free to fill in a more personal or authentic example here.) This is a long-term SMART goal for me. It's specific because I have a clear focus of what I want, which is to get my certification so that I can become a principal one day. It's measurable because I can track my progress toward this goal as I complete my courses, and I'll know when I have reached it. It's attainable because I know that it's a goal that, while challenging, is still achievable for me. It's relevant because it's something that falls in line with what I want, which is to continue in the field of education and to take on a leadership role. Lastly, it's timely. This means that I have given myself a timeframe in which I want to complete it. I am about half-way through the program, and if I continue to be successful, I will achieve this goal in another year.*

Try: *Now, we'd like you to work with a partner to think about one short-term and one long-term SMART goal. Use the template to ensure that your goals are following the SMART process.* When students are done, have students volunteer to share their responses.

Wrap-up: *Do you think setting goals with the SMART goal process makes it more likely that you'll achieve them? Why or why not?* Display the wrap-up questions and have students write their responses on a piece of paper.

Differentiation: If necessary, remind students that an acronym is a word in which each letter is the initial letter in another word, like LOL (Laugh Out Loud) or BRB (Be Right Back).

To encourage the home-school connection, have students share their SMART goals with their family and discuss ways they can help them stay accountable for achieving a goal.

SMART Goal Setting

Directions: Think about one short-term and one long-term SMART goal. Use the template below to ensure that your goals are specific, measurable, attainable, relevant, and timely.

SMART Goal Criteria	Short-term Goal:	Long-term Goal:
S - Specific Who? What? When? Where? Why?		
M - Measurable How will you know when you've reached your goal?		
A - Attainable Is this goal realistic? What do you need in order to achieve this goal?		
R - Relevant Why is this goal important to you? How does it connect to your life?		
T - Timely What is the timeframe for achieving this goal?		

Social Awareness Sample Lesson 1 *

This design and engineering challenge lesson plan utilizes empathy and compassion to integrate social awareness into your STEM or enrichment class. This lesson was written for a 6th Grade classroom. You may wish to adapt the content for your students' needs based on grade and development.

Engineering Design Challenge

Essential Questions: What does "accessible" mean? How can we design spaces in our school or community which are accessible to all?
CASEL Competency: Social awareness
Core subject areas: STEM
CCSS: ELA- RST6-8, W.6.7
NGSS: MS-ETS1-1, MS-ESS3-3
Objective: By the end of this lesson students will be able to identify why accessible spaces are important, identify a space in their school or community that isn't accessible, and come up with a plan to make the space accessible.
Approximate time: This is a project-based activity, and the exact length of time it will take to complete is flexible and depends on the time available.
Key Vocabulary: accessible, compassion, empathy, engineering design process

Materials:

- Project Plan Graphic Organizer

Warm-up: *Do you think it's important for everyone to be able to access all public spaces? Why or why not?* Display the *warm-up* questions and have students write their responses on a piece of paper. Allow student volunteers to share-out some of their answers.

Explain: *Engineering is a profession that requires empathy.* ***Empathy*** *is the ability to understand what someone else might be feeling. In order to create a design that solves a problem, engineers must first empathize with people who face that problem in their lives. For this project, we are going to act as engineers while we examine the school [or community] environment for the possible challenges a visually or physically impaired student would face in navigating the common space.*

Ask: *Let's return to the warm-up question: Do you think it's important for everyone to be able to access all spaces?* Accept student

*Adapted from PBL Learningworks.

responses and then when the video is over, ask students who disagreed if they changed their mind.

Detail: *An accessible space is one that can be entered and used by anyone.* Show the 6-minute video: Why Is Accessible Design Good for Everyone? https://www.youtube.com/watch?v=wBSy7VrGQVU. *Making sure a space is accessible isn't just the right thing to do. In many places, it is also the law. In the United States, the Americans with Disabilities Act (ADA) was enacted in 1990. It prohibits discrimination against people with disabilities and requires that all public and private places are open and without barriers for use by people with disabilities. How would you feel if you were not able to attend a sporting event because you couldn't get up the stadium stairs? You might feel pretty frustrated. Or even angry. As we mentioned earlier, being an engineer takes empathy, but it also takes compassion. Compassion happens when you are motivated to help someone. For this project, we are going to use empathy and compassion as we act as engineers while we examine the school [or community] environment for the possible challenges a visually or physically impaired student would face in navigating the common space.*

Model: *For this project, we will use the Engineering Design Process. This is a step-by-step process that engineers use to come up with a solution for a problem.* Show students the 5-minute engineering design process video: The Engineering Process: https://www.youtube.com/watch?v=fxJWin195kU. Pass out copies of the Engineering Design Challenge Graphic Organizer to students. Review the steps with students.

Try: There are a variety of ways to proceed with the project. You can have students work individually, in pairs, or in small groups. If possible, give students the opportunity to visit spaces. If materials are not available to create the prototype, students can create a visual representation. Call students back together at specific intervals to review each step of the process. Provide feedback and help students get back on track if needed.

Ask: Have students consider the following questions as they work through the engineering design challenge:

- What spaces in the school or community could benefit from the Engineering Design Challenge?
- Are there any people in the school or community you can speak to for insight?
- What creative ways can you approach the problem?

- What unique skills, experience, or expertise can you bring to solving the challenge?
- What materials do you need to develop the solution?
- What resources (financial or materials) are available in the school or community to help you put the solution in place?
- How will you test the solution?

Wrap-up: When students have completed the Engineering Design Challenge, have them make a presentation on their findings to school or community stakeholders.

Engineering Design Challenge Graphic Organizer

What is the problem you are trying to solve?

Background/research on the problem:

What are the requirements?

Brainstorm solutions.

Develop and prototype solutions.

Test the solution.

Evaluate the solution.

If the solution is successful, communicate the results.

If the solution does not meet the needs, return to the brainstorm step.

Social Awareness Sample Lesson 2*

This lesson plan integrates social awareness into your social studies/history class. This lesson was written for a 7th Grade classroom. You may wish to adapt the content for your students' needs based on grade and development.

Community Stories

Essential Questions: *What is the local history of our community? Why is it important to know local history?*
CASEL Competency: Social awareness
Core subject area: Social studies/history
CCSS: ELA-W.7.7, RI.7.9, W.7.2
C3: D2.His.1.6-8, D2.His.4.6-8, D2.His.6.6-8
Objective: By the end of this lesson students will be able to identify a local historic place or event and use primary and secondary sources to develop a presentation to inform others of the importance of the place or event.
Approximate time: This is a project-based activity, and the exact length of time it will take to complete is flexible and depends on the time available.
Key Vocabulary: bias, perspective, primary sources, secondary sources

Materials:

- Community Stories Graphic Organizer

Warm-up: *Do you think it's important to know about the history of the place where you live? Why or why not?* Display the warm-up questions and have students write their responses on a piece of paper. Allow student volunteers to share-out some of their answers.

Explain: ***Perspective*** *is the way in which we see things; our point of view. Our perspective is largely influenced by our own bias, which is defined as a prejudice in favor of or against something. A bias can be positive, for example, if you try to avoid foods that are bad for you because you want to eat healthy. Bias can also be negative, such as when you prejudge certain people based on stereotypes. A bias can be conscious, which means you are aware of it, or unconscious, which means you are not aware of it. Our bias is informed by many things, such as our experiences, family, cultural background, religion, race, where we live, gender, etc.*

---

*Adapted from Learning for Justice and PBL Learningworks.

Ask: *How do you think your perspective influences your interpretation of local events/places?* Accept student responses and confirm or correct as needed.

Detail: *Let's take a look at a real-life example of how perspective and bias influenced two women, and how they overcame it to teach others about unknown Black history in New Jersey.* Show students the 6-minute video Uncovering Mercer County's Forgotten Past: https://www.nbcnewyork.com/black-history-month/uncovering-mercer-countys-forgotten-past/2875033/?fbclid=IwAR0U5BoLdpHG QJ kEVoCmmxKK9pdk7k Oifc-FQXn92a_227_uk_IbZo. Following the video, encourage students to engage in a discussion about the issue of perspective, bias, and its influence on history using one of the Community Inquiry ideas from: www.learningforjustice.org/classroom-resources/teaching-strategies/community-inquiry.

Model: *For this project, we will be creating our own community story. The object of this activity is to tell a story about a person, place, or event in our community's history that may be unknown, or to give an additional perspective on something that is already well-known. The medium you choose to tell your story can – and should be – creative.* Show students the 5-minute video: Introduction to Storytelling: https://www.youtube.com/watch?v=1rMnzNZkIX0. Pass out copies of the Community Stories Graphic Organizer to students. Review the steps with students. Remind students that primary sources are first-hand accounts of something, such as a letter, interview, photograph, or video. Secondary sources are publications or reviews of an event. If needed, review how to create a bibliography with students using a source such as https://www.easybib.com/. If students have a difficult time identifying a person, place, or historic event, consult the local historical society, look for historic markers in the area, look through old newspapers, or look for social justice initiatives.

Try: There are a variety of ways to proceed with the project. You can have students work individually, in pairs, or in small groups. If possible, give students the opportunity to visit historic locations or interview people in the community for this project. Allow students to be creative in the way they tell their community stories. If materials are not available to create a multimedia presentation, students can create a visual representation (poster board, etc.). Call students back together at specific intervals to review each step of the process. Provide feedback and help students get back on track if needed.

Ask: Have student consider the following questions as they work through the project:

- What do you and your family know about the history of the community in which you live?
- Are there any people in the school or community you can interview for additional information?
- What diverse perspectives can you add to your knowledge?
- What unique skills, experience, or expertise can you bring to local history?
- What primary source materials do you need to learn more about the community?
- What resources or materials are available in the school or community to help you learn more about the place you live?
- How will you disseminate the information you've learned about the history of your community?

Wrap-up: When students have completed their research, have them make a presentation on their findings to the class or school.

Community Stories Graphic Organizer

What is the historic event you are trying to tell others about?

Background/Research on the Event:

What primary sources will you use?

What secondary sources will you use?

Why is this event important?

How will you communicate to others about this event?

*** Don't forget to cite your sources/references!**

Decision Making Sample Lesson*

This lesson plan on problem solving is a great way to integrate decision making into your STEM, enrichment, or an after school/club program. This lesson was written for the high school classroom. You may wish to adapt the content for your students' needs based on grade and development.

Video Game Creator Challenge

Essential Questions: *What are transformations? How can videogames be used to teach others about transformations?*
CASEL Competency: Decision making, relationship skills
Core subject area: Math
CCSS: ELA-W.9-10.2, SL.9-10.4, SL.9-10.5
CCSS: Math - HSG.CO.A.2, HSG.A.3, HSG.CO.A.5
Objective: By the end of this lesson, students will create a math-based video game using interpersonal, problem-solving, and decision-making skills.
Approximate time: This is a project-based activity, and the exact length of time it will take to complete is flexible and depends on the time available.
Key Vocabulary: decision making, interpersonal skills, problem solving

Materials:

- Video Game Creator Challenge Graphic Organizer
- Access to computers and the website scratch.mit.edu

Warm-up: *Do you like playing video games? What are your favorite video games? Why?* Display the warm-up questions and have students write their responses on a piece of paper. Allow student volunteers to share-out some of their answers.

Explain: *It looks like many of you enjoy playing video games in your spare time. That's great news, because we're going to take that expertise and use it to create a video game to teach others about transformations, which we've been learning about in math class.* (Note: You can substitute a different math concept as needed.) Working collaboratively as a team, you'll develop one game concept and then divide your game world into individual sections or levels. The trick is that each level will be designed and programmed by a different team member! Your games should incorporate multiple types of polygons

*Adapted from PBL Learningworks.

and non-polygons and different types of transformations, including translations, rotations, and reflections. Your game must accurately use key mathematics vocabulary and include a written manual for the game, explaining the game's concept, structure, and how the transformations are used within the game. User "cheat-codes" are optional but encouraged.

Ask: *Do you think video games are a good way to teach math? Why or why not?* Accept student responses and ask for elaboration as needed.

Detail: *Throughout this project, we are going to be working on creating a video game, but we're also going to be learning some other important skills, such as decision making, problem-solving, and interpersonal skills. Interpersonal skills are the communication skills we use in our everyday life when we interact with others. You'll use these a lot as you work with your team on your video game design. Decision making is the process we use to make decisions. This goes for big and small decisions – and you'll have plenty to make as you work on your level or section to complete this project! Another important set of skills is problem-solving. None of us are experts at creating video games, so it will take some problem solving for us to be able to work together to complete our assignment.*

Model: *For this project, we will be creating a math video game about transformations. Let's take a look at some games developed by other students.* Show students or allow them to explore the examples at scratch.mit.edu and provide them with a copy of the Video Game Creator Challenge Graphic Organizer.

Try: While there are a variety of ways to proceed with this project, ideally, students will work in small groups so they can focus on learning important decision-making skills as they try to negotiate problem-solving when issues arise. Allow students to be creative in the way they create their video games. Call students back together at specific intervals to review progress and provide feedback and help students stay on track as needed.

Ask: Have students consider the following questions as they work through the project:

- What considerations have to be made to ensure the game can be played by ALL students?
- What tools or resources will you need to create your game?
- Whom can you turn to for technical expertise and knowledge?

- What unique skills, experience, or expertise can you bring to the game to make it appeal to a wide variety of audiences?
- What type of help will you need to provide users of the game?
- How will you evaluate whether or not the game is successful?
- What kind of interpersonal skills will you need to collaborate with all members of the team?
- What process will you use to make decisions when the group disagrees about something?
- What process will you use to solve problems that arise?

Wrap-up: When students have completed their game, have them present it to the class or school.

Video Game Creator Challenge Graphic Organizer

What is the information you are trying to teach?

Background/research on information:

What are the system requirements?

Brainstorm ideas.

Develop and prototype video game.

Test the game.

Evaluate the game.

If the game is successful, share the game with others.

If the game is not successful, return to the brainstorm step.

Relationship Skills Sample Lesson*

This lesson plan on teamwork and collaboration is a great way to integrate relationships into your physical education, health, advisory, or homeroom class times. This lesson was written for middle schoolers; however, you can adapt it for students' needs based on grade and development.

Sharks & Minnows

Essential Questions: *What is teamwork? What is collaboration? How are they similar and different?*
CASEL Competency: Relationship skills
Core subject area: Physical education, health
Objective: In this lesson, students will use teamwork, collaboration, and communication skills to capture the most "fish."
Approximate time: The exact amount of time to complete this activity is flexible and can be adapted based on the amount of time available.
Key Vocabulary: teamwork, collaboration

Materials (per team):

- 20 tennis balls
- 1 pool noodle
- 1 basket
- Scooters (1 small scooter per person or 1 double for 2 people)
- Basketball court

Warm-up: Have students prepare for physical education class using your favorite warm up routines.

Explain: *Today we're going to play a game called sharks and minnows. This game will require good communication skills. It will also require teamwork* and *collaboration.*

Ask: *What's the difference between teamwork and collaboration?* Accept student responses and ask for elaboration as needed.

Detail: *Both teamwork and collaboration involve a group of people working together to complete a shared goal. The key difference is that teamwork combines the individual efforts of all team members to achieve a goal, while collaboration involves a group of people working collaboratively to reach a goal.*

Model: *For example, most sports require teamwork. Everyone has a role and success depends on each person doing their part. But you might have worked on a project in one of your classes at school that*

---

*Adapted from PECentral.org

was collaborative. That means you all worked together to complete the task.

Try: *Today we're going to be using both skills when we play Sharks and Minnows. Explain the game.*

- The basketball court is divided into two "oceans" at the half-court mark. On each side, under the hoop is the "shore" in which one fisherman stands outside of the out of bounds line.
- Each team has 5–7 "sharks" on scooters. Their goal is to catch the "minnows" (tennis balls) and move them toward the shore where the fisherman will try to catch them with the pool noodle. Once the minnow has passed the out of bound line, the fisherman can use their hands to put the ball in the basket.
- Each shark team has to stay in their own ocean and cannot use their hands – only their feet – to move the tennis balls toward the shore.
- The coach drops all the tennis balls (at least 20 per team) at the tip-off point and the game continues until all the balls are caught. The team with the most balls wins.

Wrap-up: When students have completed the game, ask them to identify which parts of the game required teamwork and which parts were collaborative.

Novel Studies

Just about every teacher we spoke to mentioned that they use classroom texts to help teach students about social emotional learning. The benefit of this approach is that it gives you the opportunity to integrate SEL into what you're already doing, and it gives students the opportunity to connect with the text and SEL themes.

Instead of giving specific examples of texts to use (there are simply too many to list, and we'd surely forget some great ones!), we thought it would be more helpful to provide some criteria for selecting SEL texts and some sample discussion questions to use with your students.

Text Selection Criteria

- Does the main character face some kind of challenge that is relatable?
- Does the author present a diverse perspective?
- Is the text culturally relevant?

- Is the text high interest and engaging?
- Are the characters well-rounded and fully formed instead of just a caricature of a young person/student?

Discussion Questions

If possible, try to get your students to lead the Novel Study discussions. This helps them to build ownership and typically leads to higher levels of participation and student engagement. You can use these questions to guide the discussion, but also encourage your students to come up with their own questions in advance of the discussion.

- What emotion do you think the character is experiencing? What makes you think that?
- Have you ever experienced that emotion? When?
- What other emotion words might you use to describe this experience? How might another word apply more aptly?
- What is the conflict that the character is facing?
- What events/decisions lead up to this problem?
- Could this situation have been prevented by a different course of action?
- What options exist for the character to solve this problem?
- What course of action do you think the character will choose? Why?
- Would you choose that same course of action? Why/why not?
- What attributes of the main character can you identify with/relate to? Why?
- What types of relationships exist within the story? Are they healthy relationships?
- How does the character choose to express themself/communicate? Is it effective? Do they get their point across?
- How does the character grow/change/develop over the course of the story? What does the character learn?
- Have you ever had an experience similar to the character? What did you learn? How does this learning affect your choices going forward?
- What would you say the main "teaching" or "learning" might be from this story? Why would that be important to learn?
- How does understanding this story and the circumstances that this character faced help you to understand others or yourself better?

- Would you describe the character as a leader or a team player? Why? What are the elements of a leader? What are the elements of a team player?
- How do the character's emotions help or hurt the situation? Does the character use their understanding of how they are feeling to deal with the situation effectively or not?
- Do you think the character has a growth mindset or not? Why?
- Do you think that difficult situations help you to grow as a person or cause harm?
- How did you feel about the character/situation at the beginning of the story? At the end of the story? What has changed, if anything? Why?
- Would you recommend this story to someone else? Why?
- Did this story/character remind you of another story/character? In what way?
- If you had to choose a quote from this book to represent the situation or character, which would you choose and why?
- Were you satisfied with the ending? Did it end as you thought it should? If not, how would you change the ending?
- What unique perspective does the character have? If this story could be told from another point of view (different character), whom would you think it should be told by?
- Are the characters believable? Did they remind you of anyone you know?
- If you could ask the author a question about the book, what would you ask and why?
- Did reading the story impact your mood? What mood(s) did you most experience while reading the book?
- Which part of the book stuck with you most or did you find yourself thinking about? Why?
- What character traits does the main character possess?
- What goals does the main character have? How do they achieve them?
- Is there a character in the book that you relate to? Why?
- Do you think the author is representing the character honestly?
- Are there any characters that you think you'd like to "impart some wisdom" to?
- Do you agree with the "moral of the story?" Do you think the story has an important point to tell? If so, how has the story affected you?

CHAPTER 10

Implementing SEL

By now we hope we've convinced you that you need SEL at your school and given you the tools you need to be able to do it. So, you're ready to take the plunge – now what? This chapter will help you implement SEL schoolwide, build capacity, and support your colleagues as you begin to build a culture of SEL.

Let's start with implementation.

Part I: Implementation

CASEL's helpful *Guide to Schoolwide SEL* is for anyone anywhere on the journey to implement SEL in their school. They provide a four-part framework for successful SEL implementation, which focuses on the following areas:

1. Build foundational support and create a plan.
2. Strengthen Adult SEL.
3. Promote SEL for students.
4. Practice Continuous Improvement.

Let's look at each step in more detail and within the context of schools that have recently implemented SEL.

Step 1: Build Foundational Support and Create a Plan

Sometimes just getting started is the hardest part of implementing any new program. But once you get going, the other pieces usually fall into place. When you're building a foundation for schoolwide SEL, there are three questions you should ask yourself:

1. *Who are the key stakeholders we need to make SEL happen at our school?* These individuals will be essential to the success of any program you implement. They should be

collaborative and willing to meet to discuss SEL on a regular basis. Over time, they should be willing to commit to specific roles and responsibilities when it comes to SEL. If you are an administrator, your role will be especially essential for the success of implementation.

2. *What information do stakeholders need to get on board?* Once you've identified the SEL Team, the next step is to provide them with the information they need to understand what SEL is and why it's important. Ensure that two-way communication is established and consistent.
3. *What do I need to make this happen?* Once you've got your key players, it's time to create a plan. No two SEL implementations are the same, but successful plans have several similarities, such as:

   - *They detail a school's ideal SEL vision.* This vision should be shared by all stakeholders and should reflect the current needs of the school. This vision may need to be adapted as you progress on your SEL journey. You can start by understanding why you want to implement SEL programming and identifying challenges your students (and educators) are facing.
   - *They know where they currently are on that pathway.* A good SEL plan will include a needs and resources survey so you can determine what resources are available, what SEL is already being done at the school and any other initiatives that are currently being undertaken at the school.
   - *They understand what it takes to reach their vision.* Once the information gathering has been completed, it's time to start action planning! In this phase, your team will start talking about the budget, identifying funding sources, and developing an action plan with clear steps and deadlines.
   - *They constantly evaluate their progress on the way.* Implementing any new program is an iterative process, and to ensure that you're staying on track to reaching your visions, it will be important to continue to monitor progress by collecting data and reflecting on what is working well and what needs improvement.

Step 2: Strengthen Adult SEL

Before you can build your students' SEL skills and knowledge, you must start by building the knowledge base of the adults. We're not just talking about the teachers; we mean school administrators, district officials, school counselors, recess monitors, parents, and even people in the community! There is a lot of misinformation about SEL. If you can disseminate accurate information about what SEL is, you'll have a better chance of creating an environment where program implementation is supported on every level. Try having parent/community information sessions, professional development for all school staff, and ensure that school administrators and district officials model SEL for all. Remember, research shows that most successful new program implementations in school include ongoing professional development.

Step 3: Promote SEL for Students

Okay, you've got the team, the plan, and have shared the knowledge. Now it's time to start building students' SEL skills. While it may seem that all you have to do is pick a program and start using it, studies show that for SEL to be truly effective, you need a schoolwide approach. That means more than just explicit SEL lessons in the classroom. It also means that the whole school must foster a positive climate. That tone and resulting expectations need to be set by the school administrator and should extend into every nook and cranny in the school, classroom, students' homes, and even in the community. Students and the school should live SEL all day long. The self-regulation strategy students use at school should be the same that the bus driver uses and the same that caregivers use at home.

Step 4: Practice Continuous Improvement

Implementing any new program or process doesn't happen without challenges. The same might be true for your SEL implementation. But if you can anticipate that there might be difficulties and plan for ways to overcome obstacles in advance, you'll be ahead of the game when they happen.

One of the best ways to practice continuous improvement is by organizing SEL professional development. You may want to consider doing a book study (see the PLC Study Group ideas in the Additional Resources). Providing opportunities for teachers to collaborate is also essential in this process. Finally, encourage classroom visits. This can be done on a peer-to-peer level, teacher-principal, or by the SEL coordinator. You can use the rubric on the pages that follow to help guide the observation experience.

SEL Classroom Implementation

Coach Name: ____________________ **Teacher Name:** ____________________

Class Observed: ____________________ **Date Completed:** ____________________

Please mark the answer that best describes how well you agree with each statement.

Part 1. Teacher Focus

	Strongly Disagree	Some-what Disagree	Neutral	Some-what Agree	Strongly Agree
1. The classroom is clearly a warm and caring classroom environment where SEL is being implemented (SEL curriculum is being used, posters are observed, etc.).	❍1	❍2	❍3	❍4	❍5
2. The teacher is explicitly integrating SEL language and concepts throughout the lesson.	❍1	❍2	❍3	❍4	❍5
3. The teacher creates a learning environment where students are encouraged and motivated and empowered to take responsibility for their learning.	❍1	❍2	❍3	❍4	❍5
4. The teacher uses SEL skills as part of their strategies for managing conflicts, as part of classroom procedures, and to help build positive relationships between the students.	❍1	❍2	❍3	❍4	❍5
5. The teacher models and actively promotes SEL skills and praises students when they use these skills.	❍1	❍2	❍3	❍4	❍5
6. The teacher considers SEL competencies when addressing student behavior and encourages students to monitor and regulate their behavior.	❍1	❍2	❍3	❍4	❍5

Part 2. Student Focus

	Strongly Disagree	Somewhat Disagree	Neutral	Somewhat Agree	Strongly Agree
1. Students utilize SEL language, skills, and strategies accurately and effectively.	❍1	❍2	❍3	❍4	❍5
2. Lesson builds students' self-esteem and recognizes individual strengths.	❍1	❍2	❍3	❍4	❍5
3. Activities take place in a cooperative learning environment.	❍1	❍2	❍3	❍4	❍5
4. Students understand and follow classroom norms.	❍1	❍2	❍3	❍4	❍5
5. Students understand consequences and take responsibility for actions.	❍1	❍2	❍3	❍4	❍5
6. Lesson encourages collaboration among students to improve peer-to-peer relationships.	❍1	❍2	❍3	❍4	❍5
7. Students make efforts to resolve their own conflicts peacefully.	❍1	❍2	❍3	❍4	❍5
8. Students self-monitor and self-regulate their behavior.	❍1	❍2	❍3	❍4	❍5
9. All students can access the content of the lesson.	❍1	❍2	❍3	❍4	❍5
10. Students are provided with opportunities to self-assess and self-reflect.	❍1	❍2	❍3	❍4	❍5

Notes: ____

____

SEL Observation Model

The overarching goals of this coaching model are:

- Help teachers implement quality social emotional learning in their classrooms.
- Assist teachers in using an SEL lens when assessing student's social and behavioral challenges.
- Support teachers in creating a caring classroom approach that supports the teaching of SEL skills.
- Understand that change is difficult and that observations are a supportive strategy to assist teachers in creating change in the classrooms.
- Acknowledge that every teacher is unique and has their own style of teaching and is working to support and enhance the learning of each student in their classroom.
- Realize that teachers are in a unique position to create relationships with students and that relationships are key to effective teaching.

Building a School-Wide SEL Culture

So, you're implementing SEL in your school, and things are going well – congrats! By now you may have other teachers who notice what you're doing and may want a little extra help implementing SEL; or you have a few superstars who want to up their game.

Building a school-wide SEL culture is important. The way to cultivate a school-wide SEL culture is by building relationships. And relationship skills such as communicating effectively, practicing teamwork, problem solving, and showing leadership are critical to the success of building that culture. This section will help you develop those relationship skills.

As we know, change can be hard for some people. For the experience to be successful and positive, the relationship needs to be one where both people feel safe, valued, and authentic. Let's briefly look at each feeling in more detail.

Safe

Just as a classroom needs to be safe and caring, a peer relationship should also be a safe zone. If an educator is going to be able to try new things, safety in the relationship is crucial. They must feel free to try, take risks, and make mistakes without fear.

Valued

Perhaps the most important part of any healthy relationship is for both people to feel valued. That means both the peers need to feel like they are important. Both the coaches and educators must feel like their contributions are essential.

Authentic

Have you heard the term "toxic positivity"? Toxic positivity is defined as the act of rejecting or denying stress, negativity, or other negative experiences that exist (Sokal, Trudel, and Babb, 2020). It refers to that person who is always "great" no matter what's going on around them. House is burning down? I'm great! Global pandemic? I feel terrific! These kinds of responses can be frustrating for someone who is craving authenticity. If we want people to listen to what we have to say and place value on it, then it must come from an authentic place. This doesn't mean you have to be unkind, or that you don't give the feedback at all. Find a way to be constructive and honest while delivering the feedback with care and kindness.

Positive

There is a line between toxic positivity and having a positive exchange. Feedback is a gift, and you're ultimately trying to help someone. So, try to make sure the exchange is overwhelmingly positive. Encourage them to self-assess and reflect. Solicit their feedback on what they want to work on. Together, you'll be a much more effective team, which will ultimately result in better outcomes for your students. Some questions you could ask are:

- How did that lesson feel?
- What were your goals?
- Were the class outcomes what you expected?
- What could you have done differently?

A Note About Trust and Confidentiality

It should go without saying that in a peer relationship, trust needs to be built over time through several factors. One of those factors is confidentiality. Your peers need to trust you, and you need to trust them.

CHAPTER 11

Advanced SEL Classroom Skills

Coaching in business is a now a common occurrence and it's also gaining traction in education to support professional development and career advancement. But what about using coaching tools with our students? Can the teacher be the coach? As we've mentioned in earlier chapters, research is clear that explicit lessons are the most effective means of promoting SEL skills. However, teaching strategies are also useful in helping students work through real issues they may face.

Examples of issues that students might be dealing with are:

- Difficulty with a school project/assignment
- A discussion about an academic or personal challenge a student is facing
- How to deal with a poor grade
- Navigating a peer relationship
- How to deal with problems at home
- Exploring career aspirations
- Behavior management

The primary goal of coaching is to help the student do two things:

1. Learn – either more about themselves, the situation, or about others
2. Apply what they have learned in new situations

The role of a teacher is to help a student become a positive member of their community. Teaching offers the opportunity to influence students' views and understanding. You have a significant role in helping students to find their potential and lead successful lives.

Let's look at some of the foundational strategies of coaching and how they might be used in a classroom to promote the social emotional development of our students.

Foundational Mindsets

One of the goals of coaching is to empower the person to utilize their own resourcefulness, knowledge, abilities, and innate creativity. The coach helps to support the individual in all five SEL capacities of self-awareness, self-management, social awareness, relationship management, and responsible decision making. Coaches offer feedback and support, which provides focus to achieve personal growth. By using a number of strategies, coaches work collaboratively to help the student discover a deeper understanding of their motivations, strengths, values, and aspirations. The coach's role is to be curious, compassionate and courageous in order to promote creativity and awareness, respect and trust. (Lasley, Kellogg, Michaels, and Brown, 2015) The coach also holds the following beliefs:

1. **People are whole.** Students do not need "fixing." The focus is on what has worked for them in the past and how they can build upon these skills and experiences in the future.
2. **People are creative.** Students are naturally creative. Author Sir Ken Robinson said, "There's a wealth of talent that lies in all of us. . .(we) must nurture creativity systematically and not kill it unwittingly." The coach believes that the student has the capacity to grow and succeed.
3. **People are free to choose.** Students have freedom of choice, and it is not the coach's role to be judgmental.

Relationship

The foundation of teaching is the development of the relationship between the student and the teacher. Relationships also impact the effectiveness of the teacher. The strength of connection between the student and the teacher is the difference between content delivery and meaningful learning. Sometimes it is difficult to know how to develop a strong teacher/student relationship. However, there are some fundamental elements that help to produce a safe, supportive environment, which promotes mutual respect and trust.

- Be genuine and empathetic in your interactions with students.
- Demonstrate integrity and honesty.

- Keep promises.
- Respect students' thoughts, learning styles, and their authentic selves.
- Champion your students and cheer on new skill development.

You don't have to be the coolest teacher in the school to be the most influential, trusted, and respected. By consistently demonstrating these qualities, you can build strong impactful relationships with your students. The teachers who do this well are the ones students remember long after they've left school.

Coaching Skills

Developing relationships is the foundation of coaching (and teaching). However, there are strategies that can help you to interact with students to promote the acquisition and development of the SEL skills. The role of the teacher as coach requires several skills: focused attention, listening, intuition, curiosity, and trust.

Focused attention is described by the International Coaching Federation as "the ability to be fully conscious and create spontaneous relationships with the client, employing a style that is open, flexible, and confident" (2020). When using this skill with students, the idea is to be present and not distracted by other priorities. Teaching is a challenging job, with many tasks each calling out to be addressed in the moment. However, coaching requires you to set these distractions aside and be fully present for your student.

Listening is a foundational coaching skill. Listening for not only what the student says, but how they say it, provides deep insight into your understanding of the student. Noticing body language, emotional messages, tone, pacing, and volume of the student during the coaching session gives you clues into what is being communicated. However, it is important to be aware of your underlying assumptions of these clues and check in with the student to ensure that these assumptions are correct.

Intuition refers to our gut-feelings about the overall tone of what is being communicated. As the student shares their thoughts and feelings, we can sometimes get a sense of connection to what is being discussed. Offering these intuitions can help move the conversation forward and create a shared understanding.

Curiosity is "the cure for judgment, but also the heart of learning." (Zhivotovskaya, E., 2018) A curious coach asks big questions to help explore the possibilities and options for forward movement. Detail-oriented questions might provide more information, but they do not necessarily help the student see the big picture or different path forward. This type of curiosity questioning can be challenging for teachers, as historically teachers are "knowledge keepers" and often know the answers to the questions they pose. However, as teachers enter the coaching role, they must gain comfort asking questions for which they don't know the answer. This can help bridge the relationship gap, promoting improved awareness and learning for both teacher and student.

Creating an atmosphere of trust involves a safe environment, showing up in an authentic way, being open, empathetic and with a genuine acceptance of the student. Rita Pierson's inspiring TED Talk touched on the need for the importance of trust and unconditional positive regard when she said, "Every child deserves a champion – an adult who will never give up on them, who understands the power of connection, and insists that they become the best that they can possibly be." (May 13, 2013)

Using Questions

There are several types of questions that coaches use during a session that are equally relevant when working in a classroom with students either as a group or one to one.

Questions that move the conversation forward:

- What do you need?
- What is possible now?
- What would be ideal?
- What would need to change?
- What are your options?

These questions connect to the responsible decision making capacity and help students focus on the steps of problem solving (see Chapter 6).

Questions that promote reflection help students to think about the changes that have occurred and what they might learn from these experiences.

- What has changed for you?
- Where are you now?
- What does that bring up?
- What are you noticing? (Zhivotovskaya, E., 2018)

Powerful Questions

Powerful questions help to move the student by promoting curiosity and encouraging creative thinking. These types of questions can reveal underlying assumptions, values, and beliefs that may be at play in how a student is thinking about a topic. Here is a list of powerful questions designed to promote reflective conversation.

- How have you grown this week?
- What have you learned?
- What are you grateful for?
- What could you be happy about if you chose to be?
- Does this empower you or disempower you?
- How can you have better results next time?
- Are you focused on what's wrong or what's right?
- What's the benefit of this problem?
- What does your intuition tell you?
- If you change your belief about this, what would be possible?
- Which of your core values does this goal express?
- Will this choice move you forward or keep you stuck?
- What's the first step you need to take to reach your goal?
- What's stopping you from acting?
- How would your life be transformed if you changed this right now? If you don't change this, what will it cost you in the long run?
- Are you approaching this from your head or from your heart?
- What are you willing to do to improve this situation? Or what are you willing to stop doing to improve this situation?
- What do you need in order to succeed?

Moving Forward	Reflection	Powerful
What do you need?	What has changed?	How have you grown?
What is possible?	Where are you now?	What have you learned?
What is ideal?	What does that bring up?	What are you grateful for?
What needs to change?	What are you noticing?	What could you be happy about if you chose to be?
What are your options?		Does this thought empower or disempower you?

(*continued*)

Moving Forward	Reflection	Powerful
		How can you have better results next time?
		Are you focused on what's right or what's wrong?
		What's the benefit of this problem?
		What does your intuition tell you?
		What might be possible if you changed your beliefs?
		Which of your core values does this goal express?
		Will this choice move you forward?
		What's the first step to reach your goal?
		What's stopping you from acting?
		How will this transform your life?
		Is this a head or heart decision?
		What will you do to improve the situation?
		What do you need to succeed?

Questions to Avoid

There are a few unproductive questions that should be avoided:

- "Why" questions can feel judgmental and set up resistance. They also require the student to look backward rather than forward.
  - Asking "How might you benefit from this?" will likely yield more useful data than "Why do you think this will help?"
- Yes-or no-questions shut down the conversation and don't promote understanding or forward movement.
  - "Whom can you go to for help?" rather than "Do you have anyone who can help you?"
- Leading questions are cleverly disguised advice.
  - "Don't you think that would be a better choice?" should be replaced with "If you took this path, what might happen?"

Advanced Coaching Strategies

To further hone your coaching skills, here are some additional suggestions to use in your interactions with students. Remember, the two goals of coaching are to learn and to apply this learning to new experiences.

Paraphrase

The strategy of paraphrasing is an important coaching tool to build clarity and understanding, and build the relationship between teacher and student. When someone paraphrases what you've said and shows a genuine effort to understand, this builds trust and respect. When a teacher uses this technique, students are more likely to feel heard. (Zhivotovskaya, E., 2018) Paraphrasing can also help clarify the thoughts that a student may be struggling to articulate. It's important to use the language that the student uses when paraphrasing so that the student can see their thoughts being reflected to them.

Metaphors

Throughout history, humans have used stories to convey ideas. Stories can be helpful when coaching students as well. The use of metaphors can help students understand more complex concepts and abstract ideas. The basic definition of a metaphor is when we describe something as being "like" something else. An example of this might be "He stormed into the classroom like a bull in a china shop." We use metaphors in our daily conversations much more than we realize. Metaphors help us to communicate:

- emotionally charged events
- abstract ideas
- the elements of an experience
- complex ideas through familiar concepts

Listening for the metaphors used by our students helps us better understand their inner world. Metaphors move the conversation forward in a solution-focused way. We can work with metaphors in several ways:

1. Acknowledging the metaphor used by the student.
   For example, if the student says, "I felt like I was under water during the exam," the coach would respond, "So, you are using drowning as a metaphor to describe how you felt during the exam?"

2. Develop a shared meaning of the metaphor by asking questions to confirm your understanding. For example, "How deep was the water? How cold was the water?"
3. Work with the metaphor while remaining within the boundaries of the image/thought.
   For example, "What would it take to reach safety?"
4. Change the metaphor to reflect the new way of thinking.
   For example, "This exam is an opportunity to show what you know, like a bird confidently soaring in the sky."

Celebrate

Students are inundated with evaluation in school. Assignments, homework, quizzes, and tests are a part of a student's daily life. But there are achievements that can be overlooked and often our tendency is to focus on what's not going well. Focusing on progress and where they've used their strengths can promote a growth mindset. Recognizing accomplishments, big and small, helps students reflect on their strengths and enhance a sense of pride. Celebrating as a class-wide strategy can also promote a more positive learning environment.

Brainstorm

As teachers, we often extoll the virtue of brainstorming and encourage students to think outside the box. However, as teachers, when we have preconceived ideas about how to solve problems, we set limits to that thinking and thereby limit the student's ability to problem solve. We need to keep an open mind, allowing students to explore on their own, which encourages them to take safe risks and new pathways. An unlikely idea might reveal itself to be the best solution.

Aspirations

A coach's role is to help students recall the big picture and the overall goals or aspirations. Asking the following questions may help with perspective:

- Can you look at the situation from the perspective of the future? How does the situation seem to you, looking backward?

- Can you look at the situation from an outside perspective? If this was happening to someone else, what would you think?
- Pretend that you are in a hot air balloon, rising high above the situation. How does the situation look from up there? What else can you see besides the problem?

Silence

The conversational air space need not be constantly occupied. There is nothing wrong with a little silence during the conversation to allow the student, or yourself, to ponder. Silence provides space to think. Waiting for someone to collect their thoughts shows respect, creates trust, and minimizes the expectation that the student must come up with an immediate answer.

Visioning

Sometimes referred to as "blue sky thinking," visioning helps students dream about what might be possible. Its aim is to create a "felt" experience and help students to imagine what their future might look like. Questions like:

- If you knew you couldn't fail, what would you do?
- What would you do if you weren't afraid?
- If you could create the perfect experience, what would it look like?
- If you had a magic wand, what would you wish for?

When asking a visioning question, make sure to provide some time for the student to see the vision in their mind before asking them to describe this manifestation. Adding a visioning board activity as described in Chapter 2, "Self-Awareness," can reinforce the vision and help move it out of the realm of impossible and into what might be possible.

Accountability

Goal setting is a natural part of coaching, and we discuss the various steps in Chapter 6, "Responsible Decision Making." Please refer to Chapter 6 for more clarification on helping your students set goals. The action item for the teacher/coach is to hold the student accountable for the goals they set. It creates structure, helps the student take responsibility for their goal and improves the odds of success. The role of holding the student accountable is not punitive, but rather, supportive and non-judgmental. Questions that help with accountability are:

1. What do you commit to do this week?
2. How will I know that you did it?
3. How did this accomplishment make you feel?

The coaching role is multifaceted, and the skills that we've covered above are often new for teachers. To incorporate new skills into your daily practice there are three steps.

1. **Reminder:** What will help us to remember to use a new skill in the course of our day? There are many strategies that you can use. A sticky note with the skill written on it and checkmarks when you use the strategy. Coins that you move from your left pocket to your right whenever you've tried out the strategy that day. A checklist. Reminders can be visual, auditory, sensory, or time oriented. What type of reminder might work for you?
2. **Routine:** Incorporate the new strategy into your daily routine by writing it down in your lesson planner.
3. **Reward:** How can you reward yourself when you use the strategy? Start with small, achievable goals. Slowly increase the goal and reward until the new strategy becomes habit.

As you add these coaching strategies to your teaching practice, this chart will help you to move forward and become more skilled in the art of student coaching. As you begin to use these strategies, you will move from a feeling of discomfort, to gradually feeling more confident, until the skill is part of your teaching style.

Skill	Reminder	Feeling?	Observations
Paraphrasing			
Celebrating			
Brainstorming			
Big Picture			
Silence			
Metaphors			
Visioning			
Goal Accountability			

These coaching skills can be used throughout your interactions with students in groups and one-on-one. If you set aside a specific time to coach students individually, you might want to keep track of the discussions to remind yourself what has transpired in each of the sessions. Here's a template to use to take notes and keep track of progress. Coaching notes do not need to be extensive, just a quick reminder.

Coaching Notes

Date:

Update from last session

Accountability/Celebrations

Today's focus/goal

Metaphors/themes

New awareness

Your insights into the student

Notes

Student next steps (What will they do? How will I know?)

Chapter 1 References

Buck Institute for Education's PBL Works https://www.pblworks.org/

CASEL https://casel.org/ https://casel.org/fundamentals-of-sel/what-does-the-research-say/

Education Week https://www.edweek.org/education/theres-pushback-to-social-emotional-learning-heres-what-happened-in-one-state/2020/02

Edutopia https://www.edutopia.org/article/lacking-training-teachers-develop-their-own-sel-solutions

Idaho Freedom Foundation https://idahofreedom.org/social-emotional-learning-part-2-how-sel-became-a-vehicle-for-critical-race-theory/

Nancy Bailey's Education Website https://nancyebailey.com/2018/03/19/social-emotional-learning-the-dark-side/

Phi Delta Kappan Online https://kappanonline.org/another-education-war-social-emotional-learning-debates-zhao/

Schonert-Reichl, K.A., Kitil, M.J., & Hanson-Peterson, J. (2017). To reach the students, teach the teachers: A national scan of teacher preparation and social and emotional learning. A report prepared for the Collaborative for Academic, Social, and Emotional Learning (CASEL). Vancouver, B.C.: University of British Columbia.

Chapter 2 References

Barrett, L. F. (2017). *How emotions are made: The Secret Life of the Brain.* Houghton Mifflin Harcourt.

Barrett, L. F., & Russell, J. A. (Eds.). (2015). *The Psychological Construction of Emotion.* The Guilford Press.

Barrett, L. F., & Salovey, P. (Eds.). (2002). *The Wisdom in Feeling: Psychological Processes in Emotional Intelligence.* The Guilford Press.

Grosse, G., Streubel, B., Gunzenhauser, C. et al. "Let's Talk About Emotions: the Development of Children's Emotion Vocabulary from 4 to 11 Years of Age." Affec Sci 2, 150–162 (2021). https://doi.org/10.1007/s42761-021-00040-2

Lomas, T. (2020). "Towards a cross-cultural map of wellbeing." The Journal of Positive Psychology. doi: 10.1080/17439760.2020.1791944

Lomas, T. (2019). The elements of eco-connection: A cross-cultural lexical enquiry. International Journal of Environmental Research and Public Health, 16(24):5120, doi: 10.3390/ijerph16245120

Koenig, J. (2021). *The Dictionary of Obscure Sorrows.* Simon & Schuster.

Koenig, J. Feb 19, 2016. TEDxBerkely https://youtu.be/ANFQPEkczYc

Wisconsin Office of Children's Mental Health https://dpi.wi.gov/news/dpi-connected/feelings-thermometer-take-your-emotional-temperature

Six Seconds: How to Practice Mindfulness for Teachers: https://www.youtube.com/watch?v=Hb5tM3r4nss

Mindful.org: Best Practices for Bringing Mindfulness into Schools: https://www.mindful.org/mindfulness-in-education/

Everyday Mindfulness (About Kids Health): https://www.youtube.com/watch?v=QTsUEOUaWpY

20 Terrific Guided Meditations for Teachers (We Are Teachers): https://www.weareteachers.com/teacher-guided-meditations/

Headspace for Educators: https://www.headspace.com/educators

Morning Guided Meditation for Teachers (The Mindful Teacher): http://www.mindfulteacher.com/www.mindfulteacher.com/practice/morning-guided-meditation-teachers.html

Kripalu Center for Yoga and Health: https://kripalu.org/resources/yoga-schools-isn-t-just-kids-how-teachers-benefit

Yoga 4 Classrooms: http://www.yoga4classrooms.com/yoga-4-classrooms-blog/Teacher-Burnout-yoga-mindfulness-for-teacher-resilience-classroom

Yoga for Teachers/Yoga with Adriene: https://www.youtube.com/watch?v=zRDQqJEuRcw

Chapter 3 References

Center for Disease Control and Prevention https://www.cdc.gov/sleep/index.html

Center for Disease Control and Prevention https://www.cdc.gov/sleep/about_sleep/how_much_sleep.html

US Department of Health and Human Services https://health.gov/our-work/food-nutrition/previous-dietary-guidelines/2015

US Department of Health and Human Services https://health.gov/sites/default/files/2019-09/Physical_Activity_Guidelines_2nd_edition.pdf

US Department of Agriculture https://www.usda.gov/media/blog/2013/08/13/start-school-garden-heres-how/

Center for Disease Control and Prevention https://www.cdc.gov/obesity/data/childhood.html

Mackey, A. (2020). *Emozi Grade 6 Teacher Guide.* PATHS Program LLC.

Mackey, A. (2020). *Emozi Grade 7 Teacher Guide.* PATHS Program LLC.

Mackey, A. (2020). *Emozi Grade 8 Teacher Guide.* PATHS Program LLC.

National Education Association: Shape America Blog https://blog.shapeamerica.org/2020/03/tackling-teacher-burnout-demoralization-and-self-care/

The US Department of Agriculture https://www.myplate.gov/

Center for Disease Control and Prevention https://www.cdc.gov/sleep/about_sleep/how_much_sleep.html

The American Heart Association https://www.heart.org/en/healthy-living/fitness/fitness-basics/aha-recs-for-physical-activity-in-adults

National Academies of Science, Engineering and Medicine https://www.nationalacademies.org/news/2004/02/report-sets-dietary-intake-levels-for-water-salt-and-potassium-to-maintain-health-and-reduce-chronic-disease-risk

www.wikihow.com/Draw-a-Mandala

https://zentangle.com/pages/get-started

Chapter 4 References

Atzil, S., Gao, W., Fradkin, I. *et al.* Growing a Social Brain. *Nat Hum Behav* 2, 624–636 (2018). https://doi.org/10.1038/s41562-018-0384-6

Barrett, L. F. (2017). *How Emotions are Made: The Secret Life of the Brain.* Houghton Mifflin Harcourt.

Gay, R. (2019). *The Book of Delights.* Algonquin Books of Chapel Hill.

Greater Good Science Center https://ggsc.berkeley.edu/what_we_do/major_initiatives/expanding_gratitude/youth_gratitude_project https://ggsc.berkeley.edu/what_we_do/online_courses_tools/thnx4_gratitude_journal

I Promise School https://ipromise.school/

Psychology Today https://www.psychologytoday.com/us/blog/what-mentally-strong-people-dont-do/201504/7-scientifically-proven-benefits-gratitude

Sandberg, S., Grant, A., (2017), *Option B, Facing Adversity, Building Resilience, and Finding Joy.* Penguin Random House LLC.

US Census Bureau https://www.census.gov/quickfacts/lawrencecitymassachusetts

Chapter 5 References

Atzil, S., Gao, W., Fradkin, I. *et al.* Growing a Social Brain. *Nat Hum Behav* 2, 624–636 (2018). https://doi.org/10.1038/s41562-018-0384-6

Shondaland.com https://challengingbehavior.cbcs.usf.edu/docs/whatworks/WhatWorksBrief_12.pdf

Theriault, J.E., Young, L., & Barrett, L.F. (2020). The sense of should: A biologically-based framework for modeling social pressure. *Physics of life reviews.*

What Works Clearinghouse https://challengingbehavior.cbcs.usf.edu/docs/whatworks/WhatWorksBrief_12.pdf

Chapter 6 References

Barrett, L. F. (2020). *Seven and a half lessons about the brain.* Houghton Mifflin Harcourt.

Galbin, Alexandra. (2014). AN INTRODUCTION TO SOCIAL CONSTRUCTIONISM. SOCIAL RESEARCH REPORTS. 26. 82-92.

SEE Learning https://seelearning.emory.edu/node/5

Sterling, P. (2018). Predictive regulation and human design. *eLife,* 7, e36133. https://doi.org/10.7554/eLife.36133

Theriault, J. E., Young, L., & Barrett, L. F. (2020). The sense of should: A biologically-based framework for modeling social pressure. *Physics of life reviews.*

Chapter 7 References

Association for Psychological Science https://www.psychologicalscience.org/observer/sharing-a-shift-in-emotion-science

Brown, D. (April 17, 2021). Affect Depends on Interoception. https://affectautism.com/2021/04/17/constructed-emotions/

Cherry, K. (July 4, 2021). How the theory of mind helps us understand others. https://www.verywellmind.com/theory-of-mind-4176826

Colorin Colorado https://www.colorincolorado.org/teaching-ells/creating-welcoming-classroom/social-emotional-support-ells-and-immigrant-students

Sinha, P., Kjelgaard, M. M., Gandhi, T. K., Tsourides, K., Cardinaux, A. L., Pantazis, D., Diamond, S. P., & Held, R. M. (2014). "Autism as a disorder of prediction." *Proceedings of the National Academy of Sciences of the United States of America, 111*(42), 15220–15225. https://doi.org/10.1073/pnas.1416797111

Chapter 8 References

Alvarez, J. (1994). *In the Time of the Butterflies: [a novel]*. Chapel Hill, NC: Algonquin Books of Chapel Hill.

ASU.org https://asq.org/quality-resources/decision-matrix

Facing History and Ourselves https://www.facinghistory.org/resource-library/facing-ferguson-news-literacy-digital-age/preparing-students-difficult/

Holcroft, M. (June 26, 2018). Children make around 3500 decisions a day. . .which wire would you cut? https://www.linkedin.com/pulse/children-make-around-3500-decisions-day-mark-holcroft/

Chapter 9 References

24 Character Strengths Explained: https://www.youtube.com/watch?v=OmlKBjkwEQU (9 mins)

Character Strengths 5: https://www.youtube.com/watch?v=QzyhtPTC8bw (2 min)

SMART goals - Khan Academy: https://www.youtube.com/watch?v=U4IU-y9-J8Q (3 min)

Examples of SMART goals from students: https://www.youtube.com/watch?v=R9xMTGjsZPo&t=1s (2 min)

PBL Works https://my.pblworks.org/project/making-space-change

Why Is Accessible Design Good for Everyone? https://www.youtube.com/watch?v=wBSy7VrGQVU

The Engineering Process: https://www.youtube.com/watch?v=fxJWin195kU

Learning for Justice: https://www.learningforjustice.org

Uncovering Mercer County's Forgotten Past: https://www.nbcnewyork.com/black-history-month/uncovering-mercer-countys-forgotten-past/2875033/?fbclid=IwAR0U5BoLdpHGQJ kEVoCmmxKK9pdk7k Oifc-FQXn92a_227_uk_IbZo

Introduction to Storytelling: https://www.youtube.com/watch?v=1rMnzNZkIX0

Easybib: https://www.easybib.com

PBL Works: https://my.pblworks.org/project/game-time

PE Central: https://www.pecentral.org/lessonideas/pelessonplans.html

Chapter 10 References

CASEL https://schoolguide.casel.org

Chapter 11 References

Carver, C., & Scheier, M. (1998). "On the Self-regulation of Behavior." Cambridge: Cambridge University Press.

Frankl, V. (1972). *Why Believe in Others.* Retrieved from TED: https://www.ted.com/talks/viktor_frankl_why_believe_in_others

International Coaching Federation. (2020). *ICF Core Competencies.* Retrieved from International Coaching Federation: https://coachfederation.org/core-competencies

Katie, B. (2021). *Four Liberating Questions.* Retrieved from The Work of Byron Katie: https://thework.com/2017/10/four-liberating-questions/

Lasley, M., Kellogg, V., Michaels, R., & Brown, S. (2015). *Coaching for Transformation: Pathways to Ignite Personal & Social Change Second Edition.* Troy: Discover Press.

Locke, E. (2002). *Setting Goals for Life and Happiness, Snyder, C. R. and Lopez, S. J. (Eds.), Handbook of Positive Psychology.* New York: Oxford Press.

Miller, W. R., & Rollnick, S. (2002). *Motivational Interviewing: Helping People Change Second Edition.* The Guilford Press.

Moore, C. (2020). *What Is Appreciative Inquiry? A Brief History & Real Life Examples.* Retrieved from PositivePsychology.com: https://positivepsychology.com/appreciative-inquiry/

Pierson, Rita TED Talks Education, May 13, 2013, https://youtu.be/SFnMTHhKdkw

Prochaska, J. O., DiClemente, C. C., & Norcross, J. C. (1992). "In search of how people change. Applications to addictive behaviors." *American Psychology,* 47(9):1102-14. doi: 10.1037//0003-066x.47.9.1102.

Pucci, A. (2019). *The Three Rational Questions.* Retrieved from YouTube.ca: https://www.youtube.com/watch?v=33ZtOw5YB1s

Rock, D. (2008). SCARF: A Brain-Based Model for Collaborating With and Influencing Others. *Neuro Leadership Journal: Issue 1*: http://www.your-brain-at-work.com/files/NLJ_SCARFUS.pdf

Vogt, E., Brown, J., & Isaacs, D. (2003). *The Art of Powerful Questioning.* Waltham, MA: Pegasus Communications.

Wilks, E. (2014). *Research paper: Using Metaphors in Coaching.* Retrieved from International Coach Academy: https://coachcampus.com/coach-portfolios/research-papers/elle-wilks-using-metaphors-in-coaching/

*Zhivotovskaya, E. (2018). *APPC Students & Grads: Lecture 13 - Coaching the Unconscious Part 1: Multiple Selves Theory*. Retrieved from The Flourishing Center: https://flourishing.mn.co/posts/lecture-13-coaching-the-unconscious-part-1

*Zhivotovskaya, E. (2018). *APPC Students & Grads: Lecture 3- Basics Part 2: The Agenda*. Retrieved from The Flourishing Center: APPC Students & Grads: https://flourishing.mn.co/posts/lecture-3-basics-part-2

*Zhivotovskaya, E. (2018). *APPC Students & Grads: Lecture 4 - Client vs. Issue*. Retrieved from The Flourishing Center: https://flourishing.mn.co/posts/lecture-4-client-vs-issue-part-1

*Zhivotovskaya, E. (2018). *APPC Students & Grads: Lecture 5 - The Coaching Process - The Essence of Listening & Questioning*. Retrieved from The flourishing Center: https://flourishing.mn.co/posts/lecture-5-the-coaching-process

*Zhivotovskaya, E. (2018). *APPC Students & Grads: Lecture 5 - The Coaching Process: The Essence of the Coaching Process*. Retrieved from The Flourishing Center: https://flourishing.mn.co/posts/lecture-5-the-coaching-process

*Zhivotovskaya, E. (2018). *APPC Students & Grads: Lecture 8 - Coach's Palette: Coach's Palette Part 1*. Retrieved from The Flourishing Center: https://flourishing.mn.co/posts/lecture-8-coachs-palette

*Zhivotovskaya, E. (2018). *APPC Students & Grads: Lecture 8 - Coach's Palette: Coach's Palette Part 2*. Retrieved from The Flourishing Center: https://flourishing.mn.co/posts/lecture-8-coachs-palette

*Zhivotovskaya, E. (2018). *APPC Students & Grads: Lecture 8 - Coach's Palette: Coach's Palette Part 3*. Retrieved from The Flourishing Center: https://flourishing.mn.co/posts/lecture-8-coachs-palette

*Zhivotovskaya, E. (2018). *APPC Students & Grads: Lecture 8 - Coach's Palette: Coach's Palette Part 4*. Retrieved from The Flourishing Center: https://flourishing.mn.co/posts/lecture-8-coachs-palette

Zhivotovskaya, E. (2018). *APPC Students and Grads - Lecture 7 - Multiple Agendas Part 2: Letting the Client Lead*. Retrieved from The Flourishing Center: https://flourishing.mn.co/posts/lecture-7-multiple-agendas-part-2

Zhivotovskaya, E. (2018). *APPC Students and Grads: Lecture 6 - Multiple Agendas Part 1 - Multiple Agendas.* Retrieved from The Flourishing Center: https://flourishing.mn.co/posts/lecture-6-multiple-agendas-part-1

Zhivotovskaya, E. (2018). *APPC Students and Grads: Lecture 6 - Multiple Agendas Part 1 - Two Types of Curious.* Retrieved from The Flourishing Center: https://flourishing.mn.co/posts/lecture-6-multiple-agendas-part-1

Zhivotovskaya, E. (2018). *Certificate in Applied Positive Psychology (CAPP) Manual: A Scientific Guide to Human Flourishing v3.3.* New York: The Flourishing Center.

Zhivotovskaya, E. (2020). *26.1 Hope & Change Research: Porchaska's Stages of Change.* Retrieved from The Flourishing Center: https://flourishing.mn.co/posts/1-hope-change-research

RESOURCES

SEL Indicators per Grade Range

Here are some understandings/practices to look for in an SEL-proficient student:

Domain	Early Childhood	Elementary	Middle	High School
Self-Awareness	- Uses basic emotion vocabulary - Understands uniqueness - Identifies basic feelings - Expresses specific likes and dislikes	- Understands basics of personal and social identities - Understands basics of personal, cultural, and linguistic strengths - Identifies basic emotions using developing emotion vocabulary - Demonstrates honesty and integrity - Links feelings to values - Questions bias and prejudices at a basic level - Demonstrates basic self-efficacy - Identifies strengths and has a growth mindset - Identifies interests	- Understands basics of personal and social identities - Knows personal, cultural, and linguistic strengths - Identifies emotions using a growing emotion vocabulary - Frequently demonstrates honesty and integrity - Links feelings to values, and questions bias and prejudices - Demonstrates growth in self-efficacy - Identifies strengths and has a growth mindset in areas of need - Knows interests and begins developing a sense of purpose	- Comfortable with personal and social identities - Knows and is proud of personal, cultural, and linguistic strengths - Identifies emotions using advanced emotion vocabulary - Demonstrates honesty and integrity in all actions - Links feelings to values, questions bias and prejudices, and seeks to change them - Demonstrates advanced self-efficacy - Knows strengths and has a growth mindset in areas of need - Knows interests and has an advanced sense of purpose

(*continued*)

Domain	Early Childhood	Elementary	Middle	High School
Self-Management	- Uses simple self-regulation strategies to manage feelings - Uses basic stress-management strategies - Shows some level of self-discipline and self-motivation - Sets basic goals - Becomes more independent	- Manages emotions at a basic level - Identifies and manages stress at a basic level - Demonstrates basic self-discipline and self- motivation - Developing executive functioning skills - Sets and achieves basic goals - Demonstrates courage often - Develops independence and initiative	- Manages emotions at developing level - Identifies and manages stress - Develops self-discipline and self- motivation - Advanced executive functioning skills - Sets and achieves goals using a goal-setting process - Demonstrates courage frequently - Increases level of independence - Shows basic initiative for themselves and others	- Manages emotions - Identifies and manages stress using a variety of strategies - Increases level of self-discipline and self- motivation - Effective executive functioning skills - Sets and achieves multiple goals using a goal-setting process - Usually shows courage - Shows advanced level of independence -Shows advanced initiative for themselves and others

(*continued*)

Domain	Early Childhood	Elementary	Middle	High School
Social Awareness	- Shows basic understanding of others' different perspectives - Shows basic recognition of others' strengths – Shows basic empathy and compassion - Shows basic concern for others - Expresses basic gratitude - Identifies basics of social norms - Identifies basics of situational expectations	- Shows understanding of others' different perspectives - Recognizes others' strengths - Shows empathy and compassion - Shows basic concern for others - Develops expressions of gratitude - Identifies basics of social norms - Identifies situational expectations - Understands the basics of the influences of organizations and systems	- Develops ability to take others' perspectives - Advances ability to recognize others' strengths - Shows empathy and compassion more regularly - Increases concern for others - Usually expresses gratitude - Identifies social norms and situational expectations - Increases understanding of the influences of organizations and systems	- Shows advanced ability to take others' perspectives - Shows advanced ability to recognize strengths of others - Shows empathy and compassion regularly - Advances ability to show concern for the others - Frequently expresses gratitude - Identifies complex social norms and situational expectations - Understands complexities of the influences of organizations and systems

(*continued*)

Domain	Early Childhood	Elementary	Middle	High School
Relationship Skills	- Builds basic communication skills - Builds basic relationships - Works with others well on a basic level - Solves basic problems - Demonstrates leadership qualities and works in teams - Helps others	- Growing communication skills - Develops positive relationships - Grows understanding of cultural competency - Works collaboratively in a team - Uses problem solving strategies - Resolves conflicts - Shows leadership qualities in groups - Asks for and offers help when needed	- Advances communication skills - Strengthens positive relationships - Strengthens understanding of cultural competency - Works collaboratively in a team using leadership qualities - Uses problem-solving strategies effectively - Resolves conflicts effectively - Resists negative social pressure - Offers help to others - Advocates for self and others	- Masters communication skills - Strengthens positive relationships and recognizes unhealthy ones - Advances understanding of cultural competency - Works cooperatively and collaboratively in a team - Maximizes effective problem-solving strategies - Resolves conflicts effectively and efficiently - Resists negative social pressure, identifies positive social pressure - Assumes leadership roles - Seeks opportunities to support and help others - Advocates for self and others

(*continued*)

Domain	Early Childhood	Elementary	Middle	High School
Decision Making	- Shows curiosity - Practices basic safety skills - Finds solutions for minor problems - Identifies consequences for actions on a basic level - Develops basic critical thinking skills	- Develops curiosity and open-mindedness - Practices safety - Identifies ethics - Develops judgment skills based on emotions - Identifies basic solutions for personal problems - Identifies consequences of actions - Uses critical thinking skills in the classroom - Identifies role and impact at home and in school	- Increases curiosity and open-mindedness - Usually considers safety and ethics in decisions - Develops judgment skills - Identifies solutions for personal and social problems - Considers consequences of actions - Develops critical thinking skills in and out of the classroom - Understands role and impact in the greater community	- Masters curiosity and open-mindedness - Regularly considers safety and ethics when making decisions - Makes judgments based on data and other information - Identifies and implements solutions for personal and social problems - Considers and evaluates consequences of actions - Masters critical thinking skills in and out the classroom - Understands role and impact in society

SCOPE

Use the following graphic organizer to remind students about the SCOPE Strategy when they need to self-regulate. They can also use it to keep track of other self-regulation strategies that work for them.

SCOPE

Strategy

Instructions: Use this space to write down any additional strategies that support the SCOPE Strategy you learned during the Self-Regulation activities.

Additional Strategies

S*top and take some deep breaths.* ______________________________

C*onsider how we are feeling and why.* ______________________________

O*ptions – what can we do?* ______________________________

P*lan – what are the steps?* ______________________________

E*valuate the outcome.* ______________________________

STUDENT GOAL TRACKER

Name: ____________________ Date: ________________

List 3 academic goals for the year:

1. ____
2. ____
3. ____

Check-in 1:

Did you meet your goals?
If not, what will you do to meet your goals?
If yes, how will you celebrate your accomplishments?
What new goals will you set for yourself?

Check-in 2:

Did you meet your goals?
If not, what will you do to meet your goals?
If yes, how will you celebrate your accomplishments?
What new goals will you set for yourself?

Year-end evaluation:
Reflect on the goals you set this year. Which did you meet? Which did you fall short of meeting? What did you learn about yourself from this process?

____

____

____

SEL LEARNING MODEL

Use these guidelines to ensure that you integrate social emotional learning into every lesson!

Individual Planning
Look at all five SEL competencies (Self-Awareness, Self-Management, Social Awareness, Responsible Decision Making, Relationship Skills) and ask the following questions:

- When is this child having the greatest difficulty?
- What skills can address these challenges?
- Have these skills been taught in the past?
- Does the child need more practice and support using these skills?
- What, if any, skills need to be taught?
- How will I teach these skills?
- How will I provide practice?
- How will I know when the child has learned this skill?

Group Planning
Look at all five SEL competencies and ask the following questions:

- What skills will this academic activity require?
- Have the students learned these skills before?
- How will I teach new skills?
- How will I provide practice opportunities?
- How will I know that the students have learned this skill?

PLC STUDY GUIDE

Here are some ideas and discussion questions if you're using this book to lead an SEL Professional Learning Community (PLC) in your school.

Chapter 1: Social Emotional Learning

- What is your definition of SEL?
- Why is your school implementing SEL?
- What is your school's SEL vision? (If you don't have an SEL vision statement, take some time to create one!)
- In your school, who is responsible for accountability when it comes to SEL?
- How will you know if your SEL implementation is successful?
- How is the constructionist view of emotions similar or different from your current understanding?

Chapter 2: Self-Awareness

- Why are you learning about SEL?
- What do you hope to gain from learning more about SEL?
- Complete one of the free online character strengths assessments. What does it reveal about you?
- How does your school recognize the strengths of your students?
- How important is honesty and integrity to you? Is it a key value in your school?
- What prejudices or biases do you have?
- Do you have a growth or fixed mindset?
- What is your purpose? How do you help students identify their purpose? Do you think this is important?

Chapter 3: Self-Management

- How good are you at managing your emotions?
- Do you believe there is such a thing as "good stress"? What are your favorite strategies to reduce stress?
- Do you consider yourself to be intrinsically motivated or extrinsically motivated?
- When was the last time you set a goal that you did NOT attain? What got in your way?
- Talk about a time you showed courage or a time when you saw someone demonstrate courage in a way that you admired.
- Is it better to take initiative for yourself or for others? Discuss.

Chapter 4: Social Awareness

- Can you think of a time when you really disagreed with someone and then took their perspective? Did it change your opinion?
- Describe a time that you had empathy for someone, and it led you to act with compassion.
- How do you show gratitude for others? How does it make you feel when someone shows gratitude to you?
- What unjust social norms impact you? Your students?
- What is the most valuable resource in your community?

Chapter 5: Relationship Skills

- How do you communicate most effectively? What challenges do you have when it comes to communicating with others?
- What are your warning signs for an unhealthy relationship?
- In what ways do you demonstrate cultural competency?
- Do you prefer to work alone or in collaborative groups?
- What's your go-to strategy for effective problem-solving?
- As a young person, how did you manage peer pressure? What would you say to your teenage self today?
- What does leadership mean to you? What examples of leadership can you identify at your school or in your district?

- Is it difficult for you to ask for help? Is it easier to help others?
- Talk about a time that you stood up for yourself or for others. What did it feel like?

Chapter 6: Responsible Decision Making

- Do you consider yourself to be curious?
- What does being open-minded look like for you?
- When it comes to making decisions, how easy or difficult is it for you?
- If you could go back in time, what decision would you change?
- Rate the following in importance when it comes to decisions:
  - Values
  - Ethics
  - Safety
  - Financial
- Do you always consider the consequences of your actions?
- Would you rather have a ton of data to make a decision or use an app to randomly make a decision for you?
- Name a problem you wish you could solve.

Chapter 7: SEL for ALL Students

Differentiating instruction for every student in your class can be difficult. As a group, discuss some of the strategies from the chapter, and describe how you could integrate them into your everyday classroom practice. Pick one and implement it. Report back to the group on whether you thought the strategy was a win or a pass.

Chapter 8: SEL in Every Content Area

Role-play a debate with a colleague who doesn't think they have the time or that it's their job to integrate SEL into their content-area classroom. What would you say to them to convince them that they should?

Chapter 9: SEL Lesson Plans and Novel Study Ideas

Choose one of the lesson plans or novel study ideas (or create your own) and implement it before the next PLC. Complete the self-assessment below and be prepared to discuss the results with your team:

What were your SEL learning objectives for the lesson?

What was the intended outcome of the lesson?

Did the lesson meet your expectations?

Were students engaged in the lesson material?

What went well?

What could be improved?

Would you recommend this lesson to a colleague? Why or why not?

Chapter 10: Implementing SEL

Select a partner from your PLC. Take turns observing each other's classroom during an SEL lesson and use the opportunity to learn from each other. Use the rubric and questions from Chapter 10 to guide your experience.

Using the Feelings Journal

Feelings are very important, and we have them all the time. All feelings are okay to have, and students find it useful to be able to identify specific feelings. You might wish to make copies of this Feelings Journal for them to use throughout the year to help them identify how they are feeling.

We've included a page for students in preschool/kindergarten, one for students in Grades 1–2, one for Grades 3–5, and one for students in Grades 6 and up.

To use, simply make several copies of the appropriate page and staple together for students to use throughout class. Encourage students to identify how they feel, name the specific emotion, find a definition and synonyms, and determine which reactions or behaviors are appropriate. You can use the completed pages to guide discussions in the classrooms about the nuances of specific emotions as well as similarities and differences in instances of each emotion.

My Feelings Journal

Example Thermometer

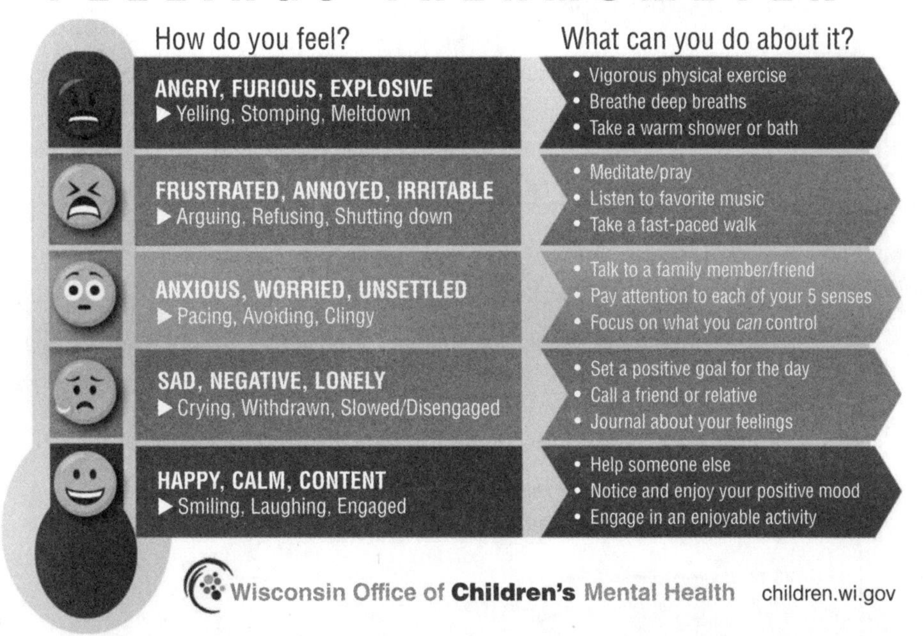

Feelings Thermometer

How are you feeling? **What can you do?**

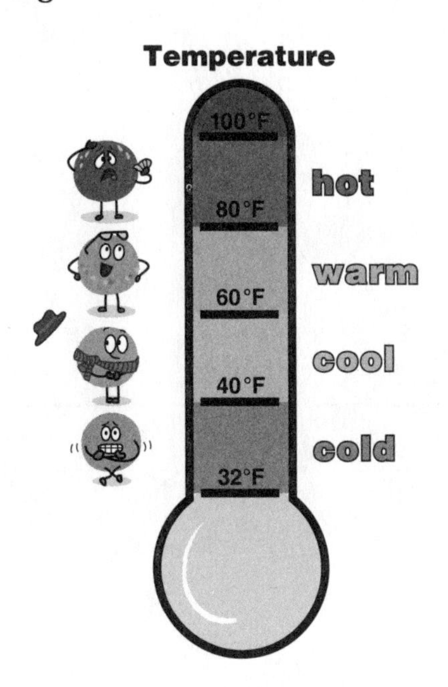

Feelings Journal

Name

Preschool/Kindergarten

Date: ___________________________________

Draw a picture of how you feel:

Grades 1 and 2

Feelings Journal

Date: ____

Draw a picture of how you feel:

Write a description of how you feel:

____

____

____

____

____

Feelings Journal

Grades 3–5

Date: ______________________

How I feel: ______________________

____

____

____

____

____

____

____

Emotion: ______________________

Definition: ______________________

____

____

____

____

____

____

____

Synonyms for the emotion:

____

____

____

____

____

____

____

____

____

Grades 6 and Up

Date: ______________________________

How I feel: ______________________________

____

____

____

____

____

____

____

Emotion: ______________________________

Definition: ______________________________

____

____

Synonyms for the emotion:

____

____

____

Another time I felt this emotion was:

____

____

____

Actions to take as a result of the emotion:

____

____

____

EPILOGUE

We commend you for taking the steps to bring social emotional learning skills into your classroom by deepening your own learning and understanding. As educators, we know how difficult the job is – especially today – and we appreciate you!

We also know that we've packed a lot of information in this book, and it may feel overwhelming. Whether you are introducing SEL in your classroom as part of a school or district-wide implementation or taking the initiative on your own to bring SEL into your classroom, remember to start small. Pick one competency per month to focus on and then gradually add the others. Before you know it, you'll have all five competencies at work in your classroom!

If possible, find a friend who shares your belief in SEL, and use the coaching resources to mentor each other. Everything's better when you have a buddy to work with!

You can also continue to develop your SEL skills. Check out our online, self-paced learning opportunities at: pathsprogram.com.

We're here to support you! Feel free to email us with any questions or concerns at: Anna-Lisa Mackey at CEO@pathsprogram.com and Melissa Ragan at raganmelissa@gmail.com.

Good luck, we welcome your comments, and do keep us posted on your progress.

Anna-Lisa Mackey and Melissa Ragan

INDEX